HOW TO TALK TO CHILDREN
ABOUT REALLY IMPORTANT THINGS

Other Books by Charles Schaefer

Group Therapies for Children and Youth
    (with L. Johnson and J. Wherry), 1983

Handbook of Play Therapy
    (with K. O'Connor), 1983

How to Influence Children: A Handbook of Practical Parenting Skills, 2nd ed., 1982

How to Help Children with Common Problems
    (with H. Millman), 1981

Therapies for School Behavior Problems
    (with H. Millman and J. Cohen), 1980

Therapies for Psychosomatic Disorders in Children
    (with H. Millman and G. Levine), 1979

Childhood Encopresis and Enuresis, 1979

Therapies for Children: A Handbook of Effective Treatments for Problem Behaviors (with H. Millman), 1977

Therapeutic Use of Child's Play, 1976

Developing Creativity in Children, 1973

Becoming Somebody: Creative Activities for Preschool Children, 1973

Young Voices: The Poetry of Children, 1970

HOW TO TALK
TO CHILDREN
ABOUT REALLY
IMPORTANT THINGS

Charles E. Schaefer, Ph.D.

PERENNIAL LIBRARY

Harper & Row, Publishers, New York
Grand Rapids, Philadelphia, St. Louis, San Francisco
London, Singapore, Sydney, Tokyo, Toronto

Designer: C. Linda Dingler

Library of Congress Cataloging in Publication Data

Schaefer, Charles E.
    How to talk to children about really important things.

    Includes index.
    1. Parenting. 2. Interpersonal communication. 3. Children's questions and answers. 4. Children and adults. I. Title.
HQ755.8.S33 1984   649'.1   84-47624
ISBN 0-06-015352-0
ISBN 0-06-091162-X (pbk.)   84 85 86 87 88 10 9 8 7 6 5 4 3 2 1
                                              92 93 94 95 MPC 10

To my wife, Anne,
and my children,
Karine and Eric

No man ever really finds out what he believes in until he begins to instruct his children.

—*Anonymous*

CONTENTS

A WORD ABOUT PRONOUNS

I have attempted to eliminate sexist language by alternating the gender of personal pronouns throughout the book. Consequently, you will read "she" in some sections and "he" in others. Please consider that the child mentioned is the one you have in mind, even though the sex reference doesn't always agree.

PREFACE

Teaching children about life in the "real world" is not an easy task. It becomes particularly difficult when you attempt to talk with your children about the really important but sensitive issues, such as sex, death, and religion. It is very difficult to respond on the "spur of the moment" to the wide range of questions children have about such important topics. At times of severe or unusual stress, the problem is compounded since parents are often so emotionally upset and preoccupied that they find it difficult to talk to their chldren and help them cope with the crisis. Wise parents, then, will prepare themselves in advance so they can handle these talks in the most helpful manner.

The purpose of this book is to aid parents and surrogate parents in thinking about what they want to say to their children about important life issues, especially at times of stress or when significant events are taking place in children's lives. What children don't know *can* hurt them. When we avoid talking about emotionally sensitive topics, our chilldren often hesitate to bring them up or ask questions about them. They may sense we are uncomfortable discussing these subjects. This closes off lines of communication between parents and children. When this happens, children become anxious, confused, and ill-prepared to cope with life's stresses and pitfalls. They may seek answers from their peers—and frequently acquire inaccurate information.

WHAT TO TALK ABOUT

Children are curious about everything. They need to be informed on issues relevant to them, including such formerly taboo topics as sex, death, religious issues, and hospitalization. Sometimes parents mistakenly think that their children don't want to hear from them, that the kids just want freedom to discover things for themselves. But the truth is that children are desperate to talk with their parents about life and death—and everything in between.

WHEN TO TELL

It is best to try to answer children's questions as soon as they are asked. If you say, "I'll talk to you about it some other time," the child may never ask again, perhaps sensing your reluctance to discuss the matter. If you haven't gotten into the habit of communicating with your children about important issues when they are quite young, it is very difficult to start offering advice when they are teenagers.

HOW TO GIVE ADVICE

Children will be more likely to listen to your advice if you follow these guidelines:

Use a "soft-sell" approach.   Offer advice in a tentative manner so that the child feels free to accept or reject it: Use suggestions or questions rather than direct orders. Children, like other people, accept and follow advice more readily when we avoid "coming on strong."

Don't get angry if your advice is not followed.   Too much pressure on a child to conform to your wishes will almost certainly trigger resistance. "Advice is like snow; the softer it falls, the longer it dwells upon, and the deeper it sinks into the mind," said Coleridge.

Know what you're talking about. To be effective in giving advice or counsel, you have to establish yourself as an expert on the subject in the eyes of your child—that is, a person with superior knowledge and/or experience. So before offering advice on a topic such as sex or alcoholism, you should read up on these topics. Your opinion will be more credible if you offer supporting evidence instead of just stating your view.

Be trustworthy. Be the kind of person who can be trusted for your honesty. Be honest about what you don't know and don't exaggerate the truth to persuade a child. Avoid distorting the truth to spare children discomfort. This only leaves them confused and misinformed. Use honest facts and figures to back up the claims you make.

Give sparingly. Give advice sparingly because even when advising is handled well, there is a danger of making a child feel dumb, inferior, or overly controlled. Don't overadvise.

Be brief. Get right to the point in giving advice. Don't beat around the bush. Be brief and state your thoughts in a few sentences. Avoid the tendency to give a lecture or lengthy, involved arguments.

Be clear. Use simple, concrete language geared to your child's level of development. Be as specific as possible and avoid generalities.

Respect your child's views. Ask children what they think about issues rather than just telling them what to do or think.

Remember to listen to and respect your children's opinions so that you talk *with* them rather than *at* them. Respect also involves giving children reasons for behaving in a certain way. Reasons help develop a child's thinking powers and independence of judgment.

Display sincere caring.   People are more likely to accept advice from someone who is seen as eager to help them in every way possible. Your children must regard you as a friend who has as a primary concern their welfare, not your own self-interest.

Avoid these common mistakes.   How not to give advice is aptly expressed in the following paragraph:

Don't preach, make windy orations, ramble, overtalk, complicate the simple, talk down, intellectualize, make convoluted interpretations, indulge in jargon, monopolize, keep attempting to convince, give a prolonged lecture, confuse through the multiplication of examples, use sarcasm, mumble, constantly reexplain, make fun of your own utterances or demean their import, hint at but never specify, endlessly contradict yourself or give double messages, never really mean or take responsibility for what you say, hesitate or tremble the words out, think aloud instead of beforehand, fall in love with and repeatedly promote your own causes and favorite themes, insist on the validity of your own interpretations, or communicate one line while living another.*

CONCLUDING REMARKS

Since every family situation is different, the advice in this book will have to be modified to fit the needs of each family. So nothing

* W. W. Dyer and J. Vriend, *Counseling Techniques That Work* (New York: Funk & Wagnalls, 1977).

here should be considered gospel or the "one best way" to talk with children. The guidelines must be adapted to a parent's belief system and lifestyle. No one can tell you exactly what to say in every situation, but general guidelines based on common sense and scholarly research can be offered. This is what I have tried to do in this book.

Comprehensive in scope, *How to Talk to Children About Really Important Things* covers a wide variety of issues. The two major sections of the book, together with some topics in each section, are: Stressful Life Experiences (death of a loved one, moving, divorce, natural disasters), and Concerns of Youth (death, sex, money, religion).

The advice in this book is directed to parents of elementary-school children—roughly ages five to twelve. These are the formative years, when children are developing the foundation for basic beliefs, values, and attitudes. In addition, it is the period when children are usually most open to and interested in receiving parental guidance. However, since parental guidance should begin during the preschool years and continue through adolescence, many topics herein will be of interest to parents of younger and older children.

Although addressed primarily to parents, this book will also be of interest to adults who work with children, including teachers, counselors, nurses, social workers, psychologists and psychiatrists.

The author would appreciate hearing from readers about your experiences intalking to children about these topics.

Charles E. Schaefer, Ph.D.
The Children's Village
Dobbs Ferry, N.Y. 10522

PART I

STRESSFUL LIFE EXPERIENCES

When we think about stress, we usually do not think in terms of children. We like to think of childhood as a happy, carefree time. In reality, no time of life is free from stress, and childhood is perhaps the time when we are most susceptible to it. The worries and fears of children are more deeply felt and less readily forgotten than those of adults who have developed greater coping skills, wide social supports, and a broader perspective based on more lifetime experiences.

Stress results whenever an event demands readjustment in one's ways of dealing with the world. The more difficult the readjustment, the greater the stress. Some stress and change are necessary for a child's growth and development. However, if stress becomes severe and/or chronic, it can result in psychological and physical disorders. Parental assistance can help children cope effectively so no lasting emotional disturbance results from situational crises.

How can parents ameliorate significant stresses associated with life changes? Just as we inoculate our children against physical diseases such as polio, so we should inoculate them against the psychological hazards of life. One

1

way to give "psychological immunization" to children is to
forewarn them as specifically as possible about forthcoming
stressful events. So tell your child exactly what to expect
during the visit to the doctor. Parents should also encourage
their child to be active in planning and preparing for pre-
dictable stresses in life. School, a new sibling, a new home,
a stay in the hospital—all are less threatening if the child
knows what to expect and especially if the child has been
a party to making plans for the event. Somehow, a new
baby seems less of an intruder to a child who helped plan
the nursery decorations, the baby's clothing, and toys for
the baby to play with. Some events are so disruptive and
demand so much change that they are always stressful experiences for the children involved. In this section, I will
also discuss ways to talk to children about such crises as
the death of a loved one, divorce, and natural disasters.

Psychologists estimate that the average individual in
our society experiences a crisis every two to ten years. The
main feelings triggered by a crisis are despair, anger, and
guilt.

Once a crisis has occurred, parents need to encourage
open and honest communication of thoughts and feelings,
and provide comfort and reassurance to the child. This
psychological "stitch in time" can prevent serious problems
from developing after a trauma.

MOVING TO A NEW HOME

One out of every five families, or nearly forty million U.S. citizens, change homes each year. It is little wonder, then, that America has been described as the most mobile of any nation in the world. Studies reveal that the predominant reason for moving is related to the employment of the husband, and that families who have moved several times are more likely to move again than families who have never moved.

THE EFFECTS OF MOVING ON CHILDREN

One aspect of moving that is frequently overlooked or left to chance is the effect relocation will have on children. Moving to a new home, especially if it is any distance from the old one, is a stressful experience for young children. They tend to like to do the same things in the same way day after day, and losing the old familiar surroundings is discomforting for them. Also, whenever we move away from a place where we've lived for a while, it feels as if we're leaving a little bit of ourselves behind. Loneliness, sadness, irritability, and anger are common emotional responses by children to a move. Some children handle the pressure by reverting for a while to acting younger than they are.

On the average, families with adolescents have more trouble than those with younger children. The worst part of a move for older children, according to their own reports, is leaving friends. Following a move, about one in four families experience distress which is serious for one or more members. If your child has trouble making friends and if one parent, or both, are dissatisfied with the relocation, you can expect more adjustment problems.

So observe children's behavior closely for at least six months after a move. In addition to loneliness problems, be particularly alert for signs of depression, such as changes in sleep patterns, appetite, and school achievement, as well as a tendency to withdraw and be alone at home, and, in older children, alcohol or other drug use.

On the positive side, a move can help children develop pride in having mastered a difficult situation. Adaptability and self-reliance can also result from the experience of moving, as well as a greater feeling of family togetherness.

HOW TO PREPARE CHILDREN FOR A MOVE

How can parents ease relocation stress on children? Preparation can make the difference between a move that is a new beginning for a family and one that is a source of real trauma. A parent with foresight will act beforehand to prevent minor difficulties from becoming serious. After you and your spouse have made the decision to move, your next step must be to tell the children. This should be a matter of top priority, since they should first hear about the move from you.

TALKING WITH CHILDREN ABOUT THE MOVE

Your children are eager to learn the same kinds of things you want to know about the move. Discuss the reasons you are moving, what the new home and community will be like, and how the children can contribute to the success of the relocation.

Point out the positive aspects of moving, such as meeting new friends, traveling, learning about a new place, going to a new school. If possible, approach the move with a spirit of adventure and with a zest for the stimulating experiences ahead. Share your hopes, dreams, and concerns with the children. Then listen and encourage your children to express their concerns and views. Be as open and honest as possible in answering their questions. Be understanding of any anger or displeasure they may express.

OTHER WAYS TO EASE THE STRAIN

Some additional ways to reduce the upset and confusion for children are:

- Include the children in making plans for the move. For example, take them with you, if possible, when you go hunting for your new house or apartment and listen to their opinions. This can reduce feelings of helplessness and powerlessness.
- Take the children to see the new home and neighborhood often if you can arrange it before you move. This reduces the fear of strangeness. If preliminary visits are not possible, take pictures of the house and bring back brochures about the community, the schools, and activities the children might join.
- Let the children help decide how their new rooms are to be arranged and decorated. Encourage them to make the new room as similar to the old one as possible— particularly the bed in relation to the window or door. The child will be comforted by this familiar arrangement of things. Try to return to a normal schedule and home routine as soon as possible.
- Don't forget the importance of goodbye rituals. Arrange for your child a special day with a best friend or a cookout for a few close friends. Children need to say to their friends that they will miss them, and to hear them say the same. Two close friends might want to exchange treasures to remember each other by. Also, take the time to make a last visit to places your family is particularly fond of.

- Encourage former ties to endure for a while. So long-distance phone calls, letters, or stay-over visits to or from old friends may be well worth the temporary additional cost. These are good ways to relieve post-move depression.

- Let the children help with the move. They can help pack their own things and carry them into the van, or carry their favorite things themselves to the new home.

- Try to choose a neighborhood with children of similar ages and encourage your children to make friends.

- Sign up your child for a favorite activity in the new community in advance of the move. Then, when you arrive, the child will not have to await enrollment time for a dance class or a baseball team. Continuity is particularly important for school-age children.

- By using dolls, boxes, and a wagon, children can get, through playacting, a feeling for the concept of moving. So encourage preschoolers and early-grade-school children to play "move," to draw pictures about it, or to collect snapshots for a scrapbook of the place they're leaving.

- Try to spend as much time at home as possible the week following the move. This is a particularly difficult time for the children.

- How effectively children manage the change of moving depends to a large extent on the support they receive from sensitive and caring parents. Children who cope best with a move have a sense of closeness with a strong family unit.

- The best time to move an elementary-school-age child may be the spring months (March, April, or May), due to a greater readiness of teachers to accept a child's former teacher's evaluations late in the year, and because the teacher often has more time to devote to a newcomer since the class routine is well established. Also, moving

during the school year rather than the summer may
make it easier for your child to make new friends.
- Provide helpful literature. Some books about moving for
  children are:

Ann Banks and Nancy Evans. *Goodbye, House*. New York: Crown Publishers, 1981. Ages 4–10.

Martha Hickman. *I'm Moving*. Nashville: Abingdon, 1974. Ages 3–7.

Shirley Hughes. *Moving Molly*. Englewood Cliffs, N.J.: Prentice-Hall, 1978.
Ages 3–6.

Rachel Isadora. *The Potter's Kitchen*. New York: Greenwillow, 1977. Ages
4–7.

Nancy Mack. *I'm Not Going*. Milwaukee: Raintree, 1976. Ages 4–8.

Sue and Jerry Milord. *Maggie and the Goodbye Gift*. New York: Lothrop,
Lee and Shepard, 1979. Ages 4–8.

Tobi Tobias. *Moving Day*. New York: Alfred A. Knopf, 1976. Ages 2–6.

Wendy Watson. *Moving*. New York: Thomas Y. Crowell, 1978. Ages
2–5.

Charlotte Zolotow. *A Tiger Called Thomas*. New York: Lothrop, Lee and
Shepard, 1963. Ages 4–7.

ANSWERS TO PARENTAL CONCERNS

The most common parental concerns about moving are:

- "Will my children make new friends easily?" Surveys
  indicate that about 90 percent of children aged six to ten
  will find it easy to make friends, while older children
  find it more difficult.
- "Will my children find school change difficult?" In general, studies show that about one-fourth of the children
  who move will find the school change difficult. The problem tends to be greater for older children. Children who
  move in the spring quarter report the least difficulty with
  a school change.
- "How will the transplant affect my children emotionally?"
  Research indicates that the transplant effect is reported

as "bad" for 19 percent of children aged eleven or older, as compared to a bad effect on only 6 percent of children aged six to ten. As previously mentioned, there are a number of things a parent can do to minimize relocation stress on a child.

A NEW BABY IN THE FAMILY

It is important to tell your children about the imminent arrival of a baby before they have a chance to overhear the news from friends or relatives. Without fanfare, simply say in a pleased tone, "We are going to have a new baby in the family." Avoid giving a long lecture such as: "You're so terrific and lovable that we've decided to have another one just like you." And don't tell a child how to feel by saying, "I'm sure you'll love and be proud of the baby."

Sharing one's parents with a newcomer is bound to arouse some resentment in young children. Help them express their mixed feelings by saying something like: "Sometimes the baby will be fine; other times the baby will cry and need a lot of watching. At times you may feel left out and jealous. If you feel this way, come and tell me. I'll give you extra loving so you'll feel good again." Also, be reassuring and tell your child that the new baby will not replace him—his place in the family is secure. If a child feels comfortable and secure in your love, he is less likely to feel jealous of a newcomer. Children need to know that they will not be loved any less once the new baby arrives.

With the arrival of a baby, a child aged one to two often feels jealous because of the drain the infant places on parental energy and attention. A temporary return to babyish behavior can be expected of the older child, such as demanding a bottle, thumb-sucking, clinging, and whining. Parents should indulge the older child's need to be babied—it rarely lasts long if the parents show acceptance and the child is secure in their love.

ADDITIONAL GUIDELINES

Some steps you can take to minimize difficulties because of a new baby include:

- Make any needed changes in the older child's routine well before the new baby arrives. If you must take the older child out of the crib, make this feel like a promotion, not a displacement.
- Keep the older child home in familiar surroundings during the birth time. Don't send him away to relatives. At best, the father will be able to take time off from work to be home.
- Don't leave for the hospital without saying goodbye to the older child and discussing how soon you will return. Keep in touch with the child by frequent phone calls. When you return home, encourage the child to inspect the infant.
- After the newcomer arrives, the older child needs to have both mom and dad to himself at times. Schedule time alone with each of you.
- Allow the older child to help with the baby's care so he feels it is his baby also. For example, the child might help in bathing the baby.
- When visitors come to the house to admire the new baby, be sure they bring gifts for the older child and pay attention to him as well.

ON BEING ADOPTED

Questions about adoption that adopted children ask seem to raise their parents' anxieties more than any other sensitive topic. Quite self-conscious about the subject, adoptive parents tend to need specific and realistic guidelines about explaining adoption to their child.

TO TELL OR NOT TO TELL

It is generally agreed that children should be told the truth about their adoptive status and that the adoptive parents should be the ones to tell them. To keep it a secret creates a strain on your communication and relationship with the child. The child is likely to sense something in your relationship that he does not understand. Also, it is difficult to keep adoption a secret. Family and friends are likely to let it slip, or the child may discover the information in the birth certificate, letters, or other papers. Adopted children become resentful and emotionally upset if they learn of their adoptive status from sources other than their parents. So adoption should be an accepted and acknowledged fact between parent and child. This does not mean that you should overemphasize the fact by bringing it into every introduction.

Studies have indicated that a high percentage of adoptees searching for birth parents were not told about their adoptive status until late in life, or were told in an angry or negative manner. Further, they were not free to discuss their questions or feelings with their parents. Adoption was just not an open topic of discussion.

WHEN TO TELL

Most adoption experts recommend "early telling"—around two or three years of age—to be followed by periodic discussions throughout childhood. Studies have shown that negative reactions in a child are minimized if you tell the child he is adopted prior to age five, versus waiting until the child is ten to twelve.

Since children's understanding of adoption changes with age and experience, you will need to keep elaborating on the adoptive relationship as the children mature, in order to deepen their understanding and answer their many questions. Only in adolescence will the child fully comprehend the complex issues involved. So "telling" is not a single event, but a lifelong process!

WHAT TO TELL

Toddler.   Start using the word "adopted" in talking to your child from age one to two years old. You might say, for example, "My darling baby, I'm so happy we adopted you." The child this age will understand little if anything of what the word means. However, he will associate it with a warm, secure feeling, and he will become used to hearing the word in a happy, loving context.

Ages three to six.   When you start explaining where babies come from, bring up the topic of adoption as one way a child comes into a family. Explain, in a matter-of-fact way, that your child grew inside another woman's body and came to you after she was born. So adopting a baby means being a mother and a father for a baby who was born to someone else. Tell the child that you want and love her as much as you would if she had grown in your body and that you always will love her. You should also explain that her birth mother loved her but felt she couldn't give her a good home. So she made a plan to find a mommy and daddy who would. Studies have shown that the vast majority of birth mothers do indeed care about the children they relinquish.

So reassure the child that she was not rejected by the birth mother or given away because she was "bad" or because there was something "wrong" with her.

Ages six to twelve. By age six, most children not only understand the difference between adoption and birth as alternative paths to parenthood, but they are apt to be aware of the existence of a third party who serves as a go-between in the adoption process. During this period they gradually recognize the permanent nature of the adoptive relationship. Questions about their birth parents often surface now. In telling children this age about adoption, stress the permanence of the adoptive relationship and the love of both birth and adoptive parents for the child.

Some answers to the frequently asked questions of children adopted at a very early age follow.

"What was my first mother like?"
"She must have had some wonderful qualities to have had you."

"How did you choose me?"
"We talked with the agency about the kind of child we wanted and they found you for us. When we saw you, we loved you and took you home with us."

"Why didn't my first mother keep me?"
"Your birth mother wanted you, but she could not take care of you because she was too young [was too poor/was too ill/had no husband]. She wanted you to have the right care, so she went to an adoption agency and the agency placed you with us, since they knew we wanted a baby. Deciding to place you with an adoption agency was a loving choice your birth mother made for your welfare."

"Why didn't you make your own baby?"
"Well, we weren't able to have our own baby. Sometimes the egg and the sperm cannot meet in a way that will make a baby."

Most adoptees want to learn as much about their biological parents as possible so as to help form their own identity. They want to know about their birth parents' looks, age, traits, talents, nationality, education, occupation. So be sure to collect as much information as you can from the adoption agency about the birth parents and the circumstances of the child's birth (time, place and type of delivery, and how the actual placement was made).

GENERAL GUIDELINES

- Be open, matter-of-fact, and honest. False or evasive responses discourage further probing. When children are not given honest answers, they may imagine something far worse than the truth.
- Keep your responses short and simple for the young child. Try not to tell more than the child wants to know. When you're not sure what your child is really asking, you might ask her to say it again or to try to say it another way.
- Your emotional tone is as important as the words you use. It is important that your feelings of love, understanding, and respect get through, no matter how you explain things.
- The crucial points to convey to an adopted child are how much you wanted her, how much you love her now, and how she will always be yours, no matter what happens.
- According to the novelist Pearl Buck, who was an adoptive mother, each period of questioning by an adopted child must be met with love, patience, and suffering.
- Don't overemphasize the adoption by saying, on introducing the child, "I want you to meet my adopted son." Adopted children don't want you to broadcast this fact to people outside the family.
- No matter how angry you get, never say to an adopted

child, "You've been so bad lately that I may have to send you back to the agency."

- Your adopted child may angrily say to you, "You're not my real parent, so you can't tell me what to do." Stay calm and state that as an adoptive parent you love him and have a legal right to tell him what to do. Tell him that you understand that he is very angry at you.
- A list of recommended books on adoption for adults and children can be obtained by sending a stamped, self-addressed envelope to: Concerned Parents for Adoption, 200 Parsippany Road, Whippany, N.J. 07981.

STARTING SCHOOL

A great milestone in a child's life is the day she first goes off to school. Each year about six million five- and six-year-olds leave home to begin kindergarten or first grade. Many more start nursery school. Entering school is probably the first major separation of the child from the secure and familiar world of home and family. It marks the entrance into a new world of learning, friendship, and adventure. Parental understanding and support during this significant event are very important for the child's initial adjustment and future attitude toward school. Children look to their parents for the confidence they need to master this new challenge.

NORMAL ANXIETIES ABOUT STARTING SCHOOL

Studies show that at the time of nursery-school entry, the majority of young children reveal signs of apprehension which may be aggravated by parents' lack of awareness and responsiveness to children's attachment needs. Consequently, many temporary behavioral disturbances have been observed in children during the first two months of kindergarten: increased dependency, exaggerated uncooperativeness or hostility, and regressive behaviors such as crying, vomiting, and bed-wetting. Children who find making the transition from home to school particularly stressful also tend to have difficulty making friends with classmates. A recent study reported that about half of the first graders observed were rated by their teachers as showing signs of stress. This was evidenced by such behaviors as timidity, thumb-sucking, fidgeting, and obstinacy. About 10 percent were discovered to exhibit signs of severe disturbance. So initiation into the school experience has been found to be emotionally upsetting for many children and traumatic for a few. Fortunately, signs of school apprehension and distress diminish significantly in most children in the third grade. In the meantime, however, many children are undergoing considerable psychic pain. What can parents do to help their young children adapt to the school experience?

PREPARING YOUR CHILD FOR ENTERING SCHOOL

Some guidelines for helping children handle this new experience are:

Familiarize the child. Explain what to expect and answer honestly all questions your child might have about school. Uncertainty tends to make one anxious, so discuss such topics as how long he will be in class each day, class routines, the name of the teacher, how he will get back and forth from school, and what behaviors will be expected of him in class (such as greeting the teacher, show and tell, and following class rules). Before school starts, be sure to tour the school building and meet the new teacher. Attend any orientation sessions held by the school for new students. Encourage your child to "play school" over and over before the actual event begins. In this way the child can try out new roles and rehearse new behaviors in an enjoyable environment.

You should also read books to the child about the experiences of other children going to school. A particularly good book is *A Child Goes to School: A Storybook for Parents and Children Together*, by Sara Stein (Doubleday, 1978). It is also helpful to buy a toy schoolhouse and to "play school" with your child over and over.

Be positive. Express a positive attitude about school. If you show enthusiasm for the school experience, the child will be more likely to look forward to it. Encourage siblings and friends to express positive attitudes also. Help your child associate school with independence, growing up, adventure, learning new things, making friends, and becoming more confident.

Expect success.   Expect your child to handle the school experience without difficulty. Be matter-of-fact and treat school entrance as something that everyone does. Don't suggest to your child that she has a choice about going or not. Be confident that your child will handle the situation, so the child can draw on your strength and calmness. Send your child off with a smile and "Have a good day at school." If your child cries after you drop her off, try not to overreact. Typically, the tears will stop soon after you leave.

Be supportive.   Children often have mixed emotions about going off to school. While they may be eager to learn and the challenge may excite them, they may feel anxious about leaving the warmth and security of home. This anxiety may cause them to cling more closely to you for a time or to regress to more immature behaviors. Extra attention and reassurance will help them over this hurdle.

Encouraging children to talk about what they might be thinking and feeling is one of the best ways to help them prepare for their first days at school. Show understanding and empathy for the child's concerns. Don't ridicule them or dismiss them lightly. Also, relating how you felt when you were their age can help children realize that they're not alone with their feelings.

Be interested.   Try to be there to welcome the child home from school the first day and to discuss the happenings of the day. Take an active interest in what your child tells you about school. Be a good listener and give him the opportunity to talk about how he feels about school and the people there.

Encourage autonomy.   The more a child is dependent on his parents for the fulfillment of all his needs and for feelings of security and happiness, the greater difficulty he will have separating from the parents and adjusting to school. This is confirmed in studies which report that mothers of competent kindergarten children tend to be more encouraging of their children's autonomous behaviors, such as walking, talking, dressing themselves, and playing by themselves. Apart from teaching self-help skills, another way to promote autonomy is to gradually increase the length of time your child is able to separate from you. To this end you can arrange for regular baby-sitters, visits with relatives, and play groups with agemates.

Make your home a learning environment.   Learning to like learning and learning to like school are closely related. So prepare your child for school by helping him to enjoy learning at home. Some learning projects and activities that you can do at home are:

- Set aside fifteen minutes each day for reading out loud—a time for just the two of you.
- Make cards or decorations together for holidays or birthdays.
- Have your child assist you in making a special dinner or dessert.
- Provide your child with an inexpensive camera and encourage her to take pictures of items of interest.
- Provide your child with workbooks suitable for preschool children.

AFTER SCHOOL HAS BEGUN

Once the initial hurdle of starting school is overcome, your child will need ongoing support. Since your time with your child is more limited now that he is away at school, plan your day so that you can spend some time with him in the afternoon or evening, or be available when he needs you.

Whenever your child shows any degree of accomplishment in what he brings home from school, praise him for what is good about what he's done. Accentuate the positives rather than focusing on the negatives. Also, help your child accept the challenge of being frustrated at school from time to time. Learning to cope with frustration is important to his development, since it prepares him to handle the trying times of life. As a general rule, try to support and help your child's development—but don't try to "protect" him from a world in which he must live. Your child must learn to solve his own conflicts with teachers and classmates.

REPEATING A GRADE

The first few years of school can be critical for a child's overall adjustment. Someone who does not compete successfully in school is likely to develop problems in living and in coping with the environment. Many children, especially boys, have a difficult time with the early grades, not because they have a low IQ or are in some other way deficient, but because they are simply not developmentally ready for the grade in which they are placed. Late-birthday boys are particularly prone to being unready for kindergarten because of immature social, emotional, and physical behavior.

Retaining a behaviorally immature child in a grade level for another year is often a wise move. Typically it is a positive experience because the student likes school better and is more confident and successful there than ever before. Often the child feels as if the weight of the world has been lifted from his shoulders.

Grade retention is not for everybody. The success of this strategy for solving serious academic difficulties has been disappointing. Seldom does it have a positive effect on school achievement. However, you can do the developmentally immature child a favor by retaining him if he is *not* ready (socially, emotionally, and physically) for the next grade. In the long run, this child's self-esteem will be enhanced, not hurt.

Of course, children must be carefully selected for grade retention. Parents should consult with the child's teachers and with a professional psychologist, who will administer appropriate tests for developmental age, such as the Gesell Developmental Placement Test. If repeating a grade is decided upon, the earlier the better. Most commonly, first grade is selected for retention since a child learns to read in first grade and repeating will help with the basics.

WHAT TO SAY TO THE CHILD

Your child's acceptance of grade retention will depend, to a large extent, on how you break the news. According to Dr. Louise Bates Ames of the Gesell Institute, parents should *calmly* tell their child that after talking things over with the teacher, they all realized they had made a *big* mistake: They started him in school before he was ready. To express empathy for the child's plight, you can say something like: "No wonder you don't like school and get tired and find it hard to finish your work. Isn't it *lucky* we discovered that you started school too soon, because now you can stay with Mrs. Grant for another year. You'll probably be one of the oldest, happiest—and possibly smartest—pupils in her class."

Or you can use the analogy of a race. Ask your child if she thinks it would be fair for her to be in a race against children who were bigger and stronger than she is. Then explain that she wasn't ready for first (or second or whatever) grade, that the others were in a way "bigger and stronger" than she was, and so you have decided that she should have a chance to do it again. Your child is likely to understand, especially if you explain that she is not being punished, that she did not "fail."

If you can convince your child that this adjustment can be a *good* thing, that the fault (if any) lies with you, that nobody is mad at—or disappointed in—the child, then the biggest part of the battle is won. Of course, you must first be convinced of the wisdom of this decision yourself. This is why the advice of child development specialists (teachers, psychologists) is so important.

RECOMMENDED READING

Ilg, Ames, Haines, and Gillespie. *School Readiness,* rev. ed. New York: Harper & Row, 1978.

SLEEP-AWAY CAMP

Ever since organized camping began in the late nineteenth century as an adjunct to a Connecticut prep school's regular academic season, summer camps have tried, through group living in the out-of-doors, to provide a unique environment conducive to emotional, educational, and social growth. Both traditional and newer specialty camps place a great deal of emphasis on group spirit and the outdoors as part of the campers' experience.

Sleep-away camp can help a child in many ways. A group living experience offers a child a chance to learn how to cooperate with others and tolerate individual differences. The routines of camp give children a sense of order and predictability. Within this secure setting, children can grow in autonomy and individuation. They also develop self-confidence in their ability to handle real-life experiences on their own.

How can parents prepare their children for an extended stay at a camp? Some guidelines are:

Do give preparatory experiences by arranging brief separations prior to camp, such as a weekend visit to relatives or sleep-overs with friends.

Do take some of the strangeness and unknown qualities out of camping by discussing well in advance what it will be like. Describe camp routines and activities, what the cabin or dorm will be like, what the bunk is like, what responsibility one has for personal hygiene, chores, etc. Establish whom to go to for advice or assistance.

Don't give the impression that you are trying to get rid of the child by sending her to camp. Rather, focus on the excitement and adventure of camping, the enjoyable activities, the skills to learn, and the friends to make.

Don't write strong "I miss you" letters which describe how everyone—including the dog—is sad and miserable without her. Don't indicate that the camper was the only one absent at a recent family cookout. Such letters will only make a child feel lonely, sad, or guilty. Of course, your child will wonder what's going on at home. Don't avoid the topic, but keep descriptions of home rather routine. For example, you might describe how the vegetable garden is growing. Convey the impression that the child hasn't really missed a thing. End the letter by simply stating, "I miss you and love you."

Do expect letters in which your child complains of lousy food, homesickness, and the lack of mail. Remember that home-sick tears are like afternoon showers—they don't last long and they help you grow.

Don't call your child on the phone for the first ten days. Let her get adjusted to camp, to being independent, to being responsible for oneself and working out problems by oneself or with the aid of the camp counselors.

Do send a camp care package of food or goodies, commonly known as "survival kits." If the camp does not allow the sending of food, send toys and trifles instead. A Camp Care Package with toys and games appropriate for children from elementary-school age up to fifteen can be ordered from Penny Whistle, 1283 Madison Avenue, New York, N.Y. 10028 (212-369-3868).

VISITS TO THE DOCTOR AND DENTIST

PREPARING CHILDREN FOR THE DOCTOR

Since routine visits to a doctor's office can be stressful to a child, you should speak in advance about which of the doctor's procedures she is likely to experience, such as:

- The doctor may ask you to step on a scale so he can weigh you and measure your height.
- The doctor may use a stethoscope, which is simply a tube through which the doctor listens to the sounds of your heart and lungs.
- The doctor may use a specially shaped flashlight to look into small spaces like your ears. This in no way will hurt you.
- The doctor may take your blood pressure by pumping up a special cuff. This will give you a tight feeling on your arm for just a short time.
- The doctor or nurse may give you a shot with a needle. The shot will hurt a little, but the medicine you get will help protect your body against germs that could make you sick.
- The doctor may take a blood sample by sticking your finger and taking a little blood out. This will help the doctor make sure that everything is O.K. It will hurt a little.

PREPARING CHILDREN FOR THE DENTIST

The experience of going to the dentist can be anxiety-provoking for children. Parents should prepare the child for a first appointment by talking about what the visit will be like. State the purpose of the visit and then describe in detail what the child will see, including the reclinable dentist's chair, the bright lights, the X-ray machine, and the tray with dental tools (hand mirror, electric brush and drill, picks, water spray). Discuss the procedures the dentist will follow. Be honest in answering any questions your child may have about the experience, including possible discomfort or pain. Express confidence in his ability to handle the situation.

You should also help your child cope with dental experiences by teaching strategies for dealing with stress. Instruct the child to relax by saying the following thoughts to himself: "If I get scared or worried I'll tell myself to 'relax' and then relax my whole body. I'll do this by first taking deep breaths and letting them out slowly, and then by tensing and relaxing different muscle groups. Then I'll tell myself, 'This is a good dentist, I'm doing good, I can handle this, I'm doing great!' " Research has shown that these strategies can help school-age children significantly reduce the anxiety and tension associated with dental treatment.

Finally, prior to a child's first appointment, it is a good idea for him to accompany someone else going for dental treatment. By observing a family member or friend handle the procedure in a positive way, the child will be better prepared to undergo it himself.

RECOMMENDED READING

Stan and Jan Berenstain. *The Berenstain Bears Go to the Doctor.* New York: Random House, 1981. Ages 3–6.
Stan and Jan Berenstain. *The Berenstain Bears Visit the Dentist.* New York: Random House, 1981. Ages 3–6.

WHEN YOUR CHILD
HAS AN ACCIDENT

An accident, such as breaking a leg in a fall, can trigger in a child feelings of vulnerability and fear of not being safe. So reassure the child that it is not likely to happen again and, if indicated, teach the child coping skills to minimize the chance of further accidents.

It may also be necessary to reassure children that they should not feel guilty or responsible for the accident. An accident should not be viewed as punishment or a sign that one is stupid or unlovable. Be sure to avoid expressing anger at the child for the accident. Parental anger can result in a loss of self-esteem and feelings of alienation from loved ones.

GOING TO THE HOSPITAL

Hospitalization is usually a stressful and anxiety-provoking experience for children, which can produce emotional and behavioral problems that last long after discharge. Some of the "threats" a hospitalization may pose for a child include: (1) the trauma of the illness or injury, (2) separation from parents, (3) the unknown, (4) uncertainty about how to behave appropriately, (5) loss of control and autonomy, (6) absence of familiar routine and environment, and (7) medical and surgical procedures. Unless these stresses are minimized, it is possible for a child to be traumatized by overwhelming anxiety.

High anxiety contributes to a myriad of behaviors that are likely to disrupt the course of healing in the hospital. Children try to ward off anxiety by denying their illness, by crying and clinging, by aggressive behavior that diverts their attention from the illness, by uncooperativeness, or by regressing to earlier stages of development. Children tend to show the greatest amount of stress and anxiety in response to procedures that involve needles (shots, drawing blood, bone marrow taps, and so on).

The younger the child is (five or six years of age and under), the more vulnerable to harmful psychological effects of the hospital experience. This is so because the very young cannot conceptualize adequately, cannot communicate readily, and have less social experience than older children. It has been observed that children aged two to four are most susceptible to anxiety.

Further, children who stay two weeks or more in the hospital are more "at risk" for psychological distress than those who stay a week or less. Children who are hospitalized for long periods of time begin to focus on their disease, and their ties to school and home become strained.

Professionals who have worked with children in hospitals nearly always agree that children who have been prepared tend to have less anxiety, and thus adjust better to the hospital, recover more quickly, and have less difficulty when they return home. Unfortunately, some parents find it hard to tell their child about an impending hospital experience. They try to reduce their own anxiety or distress by avoiding the topic. Avoidance, however, leaves the child ill-equipped for the ordeal ahead. It is better for a child to face the situation and endure a small amount of anxiety now than to suffer maximum anxiety later. Children who have been prepared in advance are more likely to experience the hospitalization as a relatively constructive time rather than a traumatic event.

BE PREPARED YOURSELF

Parents often do not possess the knowledge necessary to answer a child's questions about hospitalization and operations. So do not hesitate to ask the doctor and hospital staff for information you need to furnish sufficient facts to your child.

Information you will need includes a clear explanation of what is physically wrong with your child and how the disorder will be treated in the hospital. Find out about the specific tests and procedures that will be conducted. If surgery is needed, what exactly will be done, and what type of anesthesia will be used? What is the hospital's policy on parents "rooming in" with their child, and parent participation in the care of the child while in the hospital?

Parents also must prepare themselves emotionally for their child's hospital stay. First of all, they need confidence that medical treatment is necessary and that hospitalization is the best thing for the child. Then they have to keep their fears under control. If parents exhibit a high degree of anxiety about the hospitalization, it is almost certain that the child will have high anxiety also. So be calm and supportive of the medical personnel. Remember that a hospital visit can be a learning experience for your child on how to cope with the inevitable stresses of life. So it can have some positive psychological, as well as physical, benefits.

WHEN AND WHAT TO TELL THE CHILD

Perhaps the best way to prepare a child for a forthcoming or possible hospitalization is to talk to him about it in language he can understand. It is advisable to be as honest as possible about the hospital and any discomfort the child will experience. Discuss unpleasant aspects (e.g., needles, IVs, bedpans, restrictions) as well as the positive aspects (e.g., visits by friends, games, parents' presence). Reassure the child that it's O.K. to feel scared in a hospital, as well as lonely, homesick, and sad at times. Tell him that you know the doctor and nurses have helped other children and will also be able to help him. Talk about the hospitalization several times, since repetition allows the child to clear up misunderstandings and gradually get used to the reality ahead. Remember that parents, rather than medical personnel, should do the primary preparation of a child for the hospital. In preparing your child, leave ample time to listen to the child's concerns and respond to them.

One of the most common misunderstandings of young children is that the hospitalization is punishment for something they have done or thought. Tell your child that children do not go to the hospital for misbehavior. Rather, they go because they have been hurt in an accident, or because they are sick and need care that cannot be given in the doctor's office. Also, it is not unusual for children to fear that going to the hospital means that they will die and never come home again. Reassure them that they will return home as soon as they are well. Fears of abandonment should be undermined by pointing out that you will be accompanying the child to the hospital and will be visiting every day or will be staying with the child overnight.

When is the best time to tell a child about a scheduled hospitalization? Older children benefit most from preparation a week before, so they have time to get used to the idea, to express their anxieties, and to correct any misconceptions about the anticipated event. In general, younger children benefit most from preparation only a day or two in advance, so they don't have time to get overconcerned.

"Anticipatory guidance" involves helping children master a potentially traumatic experience such as hospitalization. This is done by telling them exactly what to expect. The first thing you will want to discuss is what will happen and why. For example, you might say, "Monday you will be going to the hospital for an operation that will help your body keep away colds and sore throats. You'll feel a little sore in your throat after the operation, but you'll soon feel better. On Thursday you'll come home." When your child asks what an "operation" is, you can say, "You will go to a room called an operating room, where the doctor will give you a medicine called anesthesia. This will put you into a special kind of sleep so you won't feel anything during the operation. After the operation you'll wake up just as you do in the morning."

At a level understandable to your child, you need to describe some of the tests or procedures that will precede the operation. In regard to a blood test, explain that only a small amount of blood is needed. If your child wants to know if something will hurt, you could answer, "Yes, it will hurt. But the doctors and nurses will try to make the hurt go away quickly." An X-ray machine can be compared to a big camera. Like a picture, it doesn't hurt to have an X-ray taken. The special picture enables the doctor to see inside a child's body and tell if anything is wrong.

A child can be prepared for admission day by explaining: "When we enter the hospital, we'll go to the admitting office, where they'll ask us a lot of questions, and then they'll give you a bracelet with your name on it to wear around your wrist. After that we'll go to the room in the children's section, where your bed will be." Also, you will want to describe the special hospital clothing, the withholding of food before an operation, where the bathroom is, the operating room and its procedures, including the anesthetizing. Tell about the pleasant aspects of the hospital, including the playroom, food, friendly staff, visits from relatives, and so on.

OTHER GUIDELINES

- Children are helped by reassurance in the form of comforting words and calming thoughts about the medical experience. Thus, if your child is frightened and cries, it can be very helpful if you make it clear that you understand how scary it is, but also how much you trust the doctors' and nurses' ability to help the child get well. Nonverbal support is also important, such as holding the child's hand.
- To overcome a child's feelings of helplessness, try to give choices whenever possible. ("Do you want to eat in your room or in the playroom?" "Do you want your temperature taken while you're on the bed or in a chair?" "Do you want the shot in your right leg or left leg?")
- Try to give your child some "coping techniques" to handle pain or anxiety. During an injection, for example, you might suggest that the child talk about something distracting or think about a pleasant scene, such as a summer vacation or a birthday party. You should also teach your child to say positive thoughts to himself to reduce anxiety, such as:

  "I can handle this."

  "It is not that bad."

  "It will only hurt for a little while."

  "The doctors and nurses will help me if I get too uncomfortable."

  Relaxation exercises can also reduce tension, so teach the child how to breathe slowly and deeply, as well as to tense and relax different muscle groups while saying words like "calm" or "relax" to himself.

- Play experiences utilizing doctor kits and hospital equipment can be extremely useful in helping the child release, understand, and master his feelings about the medical procedures. Playing with toys and with other children also provides a healthy dose of fun. Many hospitals have play specialists and playrooms with lots of toys and activities for children.
- Books with pictures and simple descriptions of another child's hospitalization can decrease the child's sense of aloneness, can instruct the child, and may answer questions she may not know how to ask. Your local librarian has many books to help a child prepare for a hospital stay. Or you can order: *Books That Help Children Deal With a Hospital Experience* (no. 017-031-00020-1), a government publication, revised in 1978, available from the U.S. Government Printing Office, Superintendent of Documents, Washington, D.C. 20402.
- Parents are the major support and security system for the child. If possible, they should stay with their child during hospitalization. This is particularly important for the child six years of age and younger. Infants and small children adapt better when the mother or other significant adult remains in the hospital with them. If you are not allowed to room in at the hospital, you should tell your child when you are leaving and when you will return.
- After your child returns home, try to discuss the things that happened during the hospitalization. If talking is difficult, ask your child to draw or paint to express inner thoughts and feelings—both the positive and the negative ones.

GOING TO A MENTAL
HEALTH PROFESSIONAL

Society's attitudes about mental health professionals have changed markedly in the past thirty-five years. There has been a greater acceptance of the fact that consulting a psychotherapist should not be considered different from seeking the services of a medical specialist.

A primary reason for preparing your child for a visit to a mental health professional is that a satisfactory evaluation or therapy session depends heavily on the child's cooperation with the professional. Without advance preparation, many children resist the visit and become quite fearful or angry about it.

How can a parent talk to a child who needs to go to a mental health professional? With young children, it is best to be matter-of-fact yet firm in discussing the appointment you have made. You might prepare the child by saying, "I've made an appointment for you to see Dr. Jones about . . . [controlling your temper, paying attention in school, etc.]. Dr. Jones is not the kind of doctor who gives shots; he is a psychologist, which means he gives psychological tests and talks and plays with children to help them with their problems." In explaining what psychological testing is like, you might say, "It's something like schoolwork. There are puzzles, and pictures to tell about. Most children like to show what good workers they are."

Or you could say, "A psychologist is someone who talks with children about how they are getting along and where they might be able to use some help. He doesn't take temperatures or anything like that; he just talks to children and has them do some things for him."

If your child should ask specific questions about the psychological evaluation, such as, "What sort of questions will he ask me?" or "What kind of puzzles will he have me make?" a good approach is to say simply, "I don't really know about that. You'll have to ask him when you see him. I'll be right outside in the waiting room while you see the doctor."

You can expect a great deal of resistance if you suddenly say, "We're taking you in for a psychiatric evaluation to determine what your problems are." It is also inappropriate to threaten your child by saying, "I'll have to take you to a headshrinker since you haven't straightened up," or "Since your behavior hasn't improved, we'll have to take you to someone to have you sent away." Such threats only increase children's reluctance to seek help, since they associate going for help with punishment.

Instead, you might say, "All of us are having a difficult time getting along in the family. We need to get some outside help to find a better way to get along with each other." Some other ways to bring the subject up are: "We're concerned about you. This problem doesn't seem to be getting any better; it keeps coming back and it doesn't seem to be under your control. We think it might help to get a consultation just to find out if it's really something to be concerned about, and if so, what can be done to help you." To an older child, you could say, "All of us have emotional problems. When we do not have effective ways of handling our tensions, when we become quite anxious or depressed, or when our behavior is very upsetting to those close to us, we may need professional help."

An older child is likely to resist your suggestion to get help and is apt to reply, "But I don't want to go see a psychologist. I'm not nuts. Do you think I'm crazy?" To this you might reply, "I understand you don't want to go. We all like to feel we're normal. Most of the time you do act pretty normally, but there are times you act troubled. Many people go to therapists, and very, very few behave in a 'crazy' way. We don't think you're crazy, but we are concerned about you and would like some advice. If you had a stomachache or toothache, we would go with you to a doctor. When there are other difficulties, it is our duty to see that you get help."

FINAL COMMENT

It is clear from the aforementioned guidelines that one should always be *truthful* in explaining what the mental health professional does and why the visit is necessary (e.g., "This is to help us find out how we can help you with your fear of going to school"), and always point out to your child that the visit is for the purpose of *helping*. Advanced preparation is essential, since most children have little or no idea what mental health professionals do.

WARNING YOUR CHILD ABOUT SEXUAL ABUSE

Child sexual abuse has long been a subject surrounded by secrecy and taboos. Adults don't want to think about this problem since it makes them nervous and they don't know what to do about it. Child sexual abuse can be categorized as either nontouching or touching.

Nontouching abuse includes verbal sexual stimulation such as frank discussions about sexual acts intended to arouse the child's interest or to shock the child; obscene telephone calls; exhibitionism; voyeurism; and letting down the bars of privacy so that the child watches or hears an act of sexual intercourse.

Touching abuse includes fondling; vaginal, oral, or anal intercourse or attempted intercourse; touching of the genitals; incest; and rape.

Recent research shows that child molestation is more widespread than was formerly supposed. In America today, statistics indicate that there is a one in four chance that a little girl will be sexually abused as a result of child molestation, incest, or rape by the time she reaches eighteen years old. Many believe that the incidence for boys is almost as high. More children between eight and twelve report being victims of sexual assault than do teenagers. It is also noteworthy that at least 10 percent of children who are sexually abused are under five. Most children do not report the abuse experience to their parents.

A little-known fact is that strangers commit only about one-third of all reported cases of child sexual abuse. Another third of the cases involve acquaintances known to the child (neighbors, baby-sitters, friends of the family, community figures), while one-third of the molestations are committed by primary relatives. So just warning children to stay away from strangers will not protect them from the majority of child molesters, who are familiar to the children and who take advantage of their trust.

At least 1 percent of girls have been victims of father-daughter incest. The sexual contact usually begins when the child is between six and twelve, and it typically consists of fondling and masturbation. Thereafter it often continues for many years and may proceed to intercourse.

Who are the child molesters? Over 90 percent are male. Many are married men who are not satisfied with their marital relationship. Others are pedophiles—adults who are compulsively and almost exclusively aroused by children. These men find a way to spend a lot of time with children and they frequently purchase books and magazines depicting young children. Most frequently they use bribery and threats rather than physical force to get a child to acquiesce. They typically begin the sexual exploitation by marginally inappropriate behavior, such as tickling a child beyond the point of a game, or touching a child on the buttocks or breast and acting as though it was an accident. Later the adult may touch the child's genitals or force the child to look at or touch his genitals.

The abuser usually tries to control the victim by:

- Coercion or using the power of authority.
- Manipulating the child into "playing a fun game" which results in unwanted physical contact.
- Bribing the child with favors or gifts.

WHAT CAN PARENTS DO?

Most parents cannot bring themselves to warn their children appropriately about the potential hazards of child abuse. One study indicated that only 29 percent of parents talk explicitly about sexual abuse or child molestation with their children. Even fewer mentioned that abuse could be initiated by a member of their own family. In general, parents are telling their children too little, too late (after age nine).

Don't wait until your child asks you about this danger. Children need to be forewarned about the possibility of sexual abuse; otherwise they may not be able to cope because of uncertainty, shame, or confusion. So don't let your children be taken totally by surprise. You can improve their chances by helping them to recognize and avoid troublesome circumstances. You need to tell them specifically what might happen, and what steps they can take to protect themselves. It is best to warn children about sexual abuse as soon as they can understand, which is often by the age of four. However, rational, instructive discussions can begin at any age.

Experience has shown that children can be made aware of sexual abuse in a way that will not frighten them unduly. Be straightforward and reassuring in giving them the facts. Discuss this problem within a context of safety information in general: safety in crossing the streets, safety in avoiding poisons around the house, and safety involving people who might want to touch them in the wrong way. In this manner, children will learn that this is one of a variety of survival skills they should know about.

WHAT TO SAY

Just what you say will depend on your child's age. The goal is the same: to give your children enough specific, accurate information to recognize sexually abusive behavior, and some ways to handle potentially dangérous situations.

To explain to a school age child what sexual abuse is, you might say something like one of the following:

"Someday you may meet an adult who may try to touch your 'private parts'—the parts of your body covered by underwear. These parts of your body are off limits to other people. A person may try to put his hand down your shirt or pants. It is wrong for the person to do this and you should try to get away from him. This person may be a stranger or someone you know. It is also possible that you will see a man who exposes himself by showing his penis. He might be in a car, or on the sidewalk.

He's trying to scare someone. What you need to do is get away from him, and tell someone about him quickly. Tell me, and the police will want to know too, because this is against the law."

"Some adults may offer you candy or presents to do sexual things with them, and then ask you to keep it secret. It is not O.K. for you to keep secrets about that sort of thing."

"I want you to know that older people don't have the right to do anything they want with children. One of the things they don't have a right to do is to touch children's bodies in private areas or to ask children to touch them in such places or to expose themselves [undress] in the presence of children."

"It's possible that someone may try to take advantage of you. Don't let anyone touch your penis. I want you to say 'No' and then tell me about it if someone tries this."

"If some older person asks you to undress or wants to touch your private parts, say 'No' and come home and tell us right away."

"Sometimes big people will do things that aren't right, like try to touch children's private parts. I want you to tell me if this ever happens."

SELF-PROTECTION

Some ways to teach your child to avoid dangers are to say: "Don't play alone in deserted areas or use public rest rooms alone." "Don't go near strangers—which means any person you don't know—even if he seems friendly." "Don't accept candy, rides, or other treats or activities—like 'Come see my kitten'—from an unknown adult. Rather, pay no attention to the offer and walk away quickly. Don't believe a stranger who says, 'Your mom sent me to walk with you.' I will never send a stranger to pick you up." "When home alone, don't open the door at all or talk to unfamiliar callers on the phone."

You should also tell your child what to do if approached. Many times a traumatic incident can be stopped by a child saying "No!" in a firm way and quickly moving away. You can help your child rehearse phrases to use, such as: "No, don't do that." "I'll tell my mother." "No, I can't do that. My parents told me not to." "Stop! That's not O.K.!" If there is another adult nearby, the child should seek help right away. Of course, if an adult is threatening with a knife or gun, the child should realize that active resistance probably would not be wise.

REHEARSAL

Help your children develop problem-solving skills by asking what they would do in a variety of dangerous situations. Make up "What if" games, saying to a child: "What if a strange man, claiming to be a policeman, tells you to get into his car so he can ask you questions. What would you do?" "What if a friend or relative wants to put his hand down your pants. What would you do?" "What if a stranger offers you money to do something for him?"

You should also have realistic discussions of stories in newspapers and on TV about actual child sexual abuse incidents, such as a young hitchhiker who was sexually assaulted. Any personal experiences you had as a child should be related as well.

OTHER GUIDELINES

- Be sure you have given your children a good sex education from an early age. The more they are informed about human sexuality, the less an offender can capitalize on their ignorance or curiosity to engage them in sex. Children should know the proper names and functions for genitalia, because this makes them discussible and understandable. Children should also be taught that sexual assault is a violent and mean thing, while sex itself is a beautiful thing.
- Be sure your children feel comfortable talking openly to you about sensitive topics in general.

- You cannot effectively warn a child about sexual abuse through one discussion. Repetition is important in order that children learn, so repeat your instructions, using different wording at different times. After a discussion with a child, you might follow up a few days later with a question about whether the child has thought about it anymore.

- Children should understand the difference between a "good" and a "bad" touch. A good touch is tender and loving and makes you feel as if something has been given. A bad touch hurts, makes you feel bad, "funny," or as if something has been taken from you. So explain the difference between affectionate and exploitative touching.

- Whenever your child tells you she has handled a potentially dangerous situation in an appropriate way, be sure to praise the child and express your approval. You might say, for example, "You did so well to get out of that house when the man was pressuring you to stay."

- You can minimize opportunities for child sexual abuse by closely supervising your child's activities—know where and with whom the child spends her time and what activities are engaged in. Do not leave your child unsupervised for a long period of time, even in a supposedly "safe" place.

Some parents have tried to head off the possibility of child molestation by teaching their children a code word and telling them never to go off with anyone who does not know the code word.

WHEN YOUR CHILD IS A VICTIM OF SEXUAL ABUSE

The typical victim of sexual abuse is a white girl, nine years old, from a working-class family. She was abused by an adult male relative, usually her father. With boys, abuse is most often by a male agemate. Genital abuse is the most frequent type of sexual abuse. Close to two-thirds of all children who are victimized may not tell their parents or anyone else about it.

CHILDREN'S REACTIONS

Clinical studies of sexually abused children reveal psychological suffering among virtually all of them—most of it at moderate levels. Typical symptoms of abused children include generalized fear and mistrust, sadness, feelings of guilt and shame, and a feeling of being "different" or contaminated by the abnormal sexual experience. The child may regress to an earlier stage of development and start to bed-wet, thumb-suck, or show separation anxiety, sleeping and eating difficulties. For a time, the child may have a strong aversion to being touched, even by her parents. Some show psychosomatic disorders, aggressive behaviors, and learning problems. These are usually temporary reactions that will subside in a few weeks. If no violence or incest was involved, you can probably handle the situation yourself by being understanding and supportive. Psychotherapy may be needed if the child is not adapting well after a couple of months have passed.

WHAT CAN PARENTS DO?

Few parents are prepared to deal with a situation where someone has sexually abused their child. There is a natural reluctance to confront such a painful and disturbing event. Since the abuse usually does not involve actual intercourse, parents tend to breathe a sigh of relief and convince themselves that "nothing really happened." But any form of molestation can be a stressful experience for a child, since it is done in an atmosphere of exploitation or violence. How parents handle the situation may determine if there is a lasting traumatic effect on the child.

The victim of child sexual abuse needs parents who can help her regain a sense of control, safety, and self-esteem. From the victim state, the child needs to move to a more active, coping role. The following are some important steps you can take to help your child deal with the experience.

Encourage the child to "talk it out." The more a child can talk about the experience, the more control she will gain over it. Talking about the incident is therapeutic for most children. The incident is not forgotten, even if it is not discussed. Children can benefit from expressing themselves with words, tears, drawings, dolls, and puppets—whatever helps them share their experience. Let your child know that it is O.K. to talk about it. Be a good listener and help the child express any feelings of fear, anger, humiliation, guilt, confusion, or embarrassment. The child may need to talk about it again and again before being able to assimilate the experience.

Believe the child. It is very important for you to believe the child when she reports an incidence of sexual abuse. Professional experience indicates that children do not fabricate this type of story. Don't deny the incident by saying, "Oh, you just imagined that," or "Stop making up stories!" Even if the incident involves a friend or relative, you must face up to the reality of it.

　　　Praise the child for reporting it.　Assure your child that she did absolutely the right thing in telling you about the incident. Most molesters either cajole or threaten the child into keeping the episode a secret.

　　　Relieve the child of blame.　Be very clear about the fact that you believe the responsibility and blame for the act rests solely with the adult. You might describe the molester as "sick" or "mixed up." It is never the child's fault; so don't say, "How could you let this happen to you?" It is the attacker who must bear the responsibility for this demeaning act.

　　　Comfort the child.　Give emotional first aid by reassuring the child of your love and offering comfort. Say you are sorry that something like this happened, but do not express so much distress that your child gets the impression that this is the worst thing that could possibly have happened to her. The proper reaction is one of tenderness and sympathy—not pity.

　　　Control your emotions.　Most of us feel outrage and anger when a child has been victimized. You should discuss your feelings of anger or guilt with another adult, not with your child. In this way the child will not assume responsibility for these feelings or be frightened because she believes the feelings are directed at her.

　　　Promise protection from further abuse.　Tell your child that you are going to do everything possible to see that this does not happen again. If the offender is a stranger, simply report the matter to the police. By making a report, you give your child a greater sense of control and decrease the feeling of having been victimized.

If the molester is a friend or relative, you will want to confront him about it, and you may also decide to report it to the police or the social agency designated by state law to protect children from abuse. In deciding whether to report a friend or relative, remember that research shows that sexual molestation is seldom a one-time offense. Being caught and being forced to receive professional help may be the best thing for an offender in the long run.

Parents who have reported a sexual abuse incident have generally found that a child's distress decreases rather than increases. It seems to give a child a sense of being an active problem-solver rather than a passive victim.

TALKING WITH A CRITICALLY ILL CHILD

The fatal illness of a child is a devastating experience for parents. Dr. Elisabeth Kübler-Ross, an expert on dying, has described five stages of response which parents can expect to go through when they realize their child is dying.

Characteristically, the parents of the dying child show an initial reaction of denial. When the early feelings of denial cannot be maintained any longer, they are replaced by manifestations of anger and rage, often vented at God or the physician. As the parents come to realize that anger has not changed the unacceptable reality, there is a tendency to revert to a device frequently used by children, bargaining. They may promise to abandon venality or to undertake heroic service, placating God or benefiting mankind, in return for a cure or a temporary prolongation of life. When the parents of the terminally ill child can no longer effectively deny the seriousness of the illness, depressive symptoms usually develop. In the beginning, the parents are depressed about their child's suffering and disfigurement, if any. As time goes on, another type of depression develops, resulting from the grief the parents feel in preparing for the final separation from the child. If parents have had enough time and help in working through these various stages, they will contemplate the coming end with a degree of quiet expectation. Acceptance should not be mistaken for happiness, but be perceived as a near-void of feelings. It is as if the pain is gone, the struggle over, and there is time for a rest before the child's final journey. It is difficult for many parents to reach this final stage of acceptance.

Children are often far ahead of their families in dealing with their impending death. According to Kübler-Ross, it is beautiful how children can accept death if they have an adult who is supportive and can talk about it without making it a nightmare

Anxious to protect a fatally ill child, many parents do not tell the child of the nature and severity of her illness. But most fatally ill children aged six and over sense that they are very ill and that they could die from it. They are eager to have their parents help them talk about their illness, death, and dying.

The fears of fatally ill children will vary with age. Up until about age five, the child fears separation from her parents more than death. The six-to-nine-year-old child fears the pain of dying or the physical assault of hospital procedures. The older child understands the reality of death and fears this the most.

BE HONEST WITH THE CRITICALLY ILL CHILD

Research indicates that critically ill children sense the deep distress of their parents and the medical staff despite the adults' efforts to behave in a cheerful, normal manner. Children as young as six years of age, if afflicted with cancer, become aware that they have no ordinary illness, even when no one tells them about it. They perceive that they have a very serious illness and eventually they realize they might die from it.

Families whose child over six died of a serious illness report that open communication about the illness resulted in an increased feeling of closeness to the child. Families whose children died without open discussion of the illness or of the imminent death usually report that they wish they had spoken more openly with their child. These parents describe feelings of incompleteness and of not having had the chance to say goodbye. An honest discussion with the child of the diagnosis and prognosis early on seems to result in better psychological adjustment by the child and by family members.* Open communication with a child about the illness and his concerns can help decrease feelings of isolation, fear, and loneliness.

* L. A. Slavin et al. "Communication of the Cancer Diagnosis to Pediatric Patients: Impact on Long-term Adjustment," *American Journal of Psychiatry* 139 (1982): 179–183.

Many children will want to discuss their approaching death. If the child brings it up, you should try to discuss it with honesty, love, and acceptance. Truth is more supportive and beneficial to a child than deception or denial. If a seriously ill child asks if he's going to die, you might answer, "I can understand that you worry you might die. I have thought about it too. You have a serious illness, but right now the doctors tell us that there are still things to do and medicines to take that can make you feel better." When the child is very close to death and there is *clearly* no hope left, and the child asks about dying, you should tell him that the doctors have no further way of curing the sickness, but they will make sure he will be comfortable until he dies. If you are religious, you could tell the child, "You will be going to a new life in heaven—one of happiness, peace, and love."

DEATH OF A
LOVED ONE

Living through the loss of a loved one can have positive and maturing aspects. Life consists of many separations and losses, and an early loss can prepare a child for later traumas.

The greatest loss of all for a child is the death of a parent. Each year there are about a half-million children who suffer the death of a parent. The surviving parent, desiring to protect the children, may try to shield them from experiencing the loss, expressing grief, and sharing in the family's mourning. But children have the same need as adults to mourn and to realize what has happened.

There are five basic needs in all children of all ages when faced with the death of a parent:

- The need for information that is clear and comprehensible.
- The need to feel involved and important.
- The need for reassurance about the grief of adults around them.
- The need for their own thoughts and feelings.
- The need to maintain their own age-appropriate interests and activities.

If a family member is dying, the news is best told by a parent. If at all possible, however, the child should be allowed to talk directly with the dying loved one, so that child and adult can share their feelings and say loving farewells.

The child should be told as promptly and simply as possible about what has happened, and be allowed to ask all sorts of questions and have them answered as honestly as possible.

In telling the child about the death, try to communicate by your touch (holding her on your lap, or stroking her soothingly with your hand) that she is not alone in this, that you are there.

When possible, begin by talking about things the child has experienced or noticed already: "As you knew, Mommy has been very sick lately and has had to go to the hospital several times." Next, give the facts of the death: "The doctor just called to tell us that Mom died this morning."

Reassure the child that although you are sad and upset, you are strong and will be able to take care of him. Explain that the death was not his fault and that there was nothing he could have done—or can do—to make things different.

If the child asks if you will die too, reassure him that you are likely to live a long life and that he will no doubt be grown up and have his own family by the time you die. Speak of who is available to take care of the child in the unlikely event of your dying. Don't send your child away at this time; this can only increase fears of abandonment and wild fantasies about what has happened.

HOW A DYING PARENT CAN HELP

A dying parent has a unique opportunity to prepare the child for the impending death. When possible, the child should be allowed continual and reasonable contact with the parent, along with opportunities to "do for" the parent so the child can feel he is doing something to relieve the pain and suffering. Preventing children from visiting a fatally ill parent in the hospital does not protect them; on the contrary, it can lead to feelings of abandonment or the development of frightening fantasies. School-age children will not be overwhelmed by seeing a sick parent if they have received adequate preparation and support. Simple and specific explanations of what the child will see can lessen fear. It is important to describe hospital equipment and machines in terms of the helpful role they play (e.g., "The tube in Daddy's arm gives him food because he feels too sick to eat"). Equipment such as a syringe or a blood pressure gauge tubing can be given to children to inspect so that they can become familiar and comfortable with the hospital environment. If the sick parent's appearance is notably different, point this out and relate it to the disease process. The child should be encouraged to go physically close to the parent when possible; sitting on the bed, touching, and hugging can help normalize the situation and make it less strange.

The dying parent should also reassure the child of continuing love, while explaining death in terms geared toward the child's level of comprehension. A beautiful example of a dying mother's loving response to her eleven-year-old son was given in return to his request that she ask his father not to remarry following her death. She replied:

"I would not want Daddy to make such a promise. You see, people who have had a happy marriage, as Dad and I have had, are the ones who will want to remarry. They know how to love and how much loving can bring to their lives. So Dad will eventually want to remarry and it will be a tribute to me and to our long marriage."*

BEREAVEMENT

Bereavement (loss of a loved one through death) is a traumatic experience for people of all ages. After a loss, it's natural to experience grief, which involves both psychological and physiological reactions of sorrow. The first stage of grief is one of *numbness,* wherein one tends to be in shock, as if suspended in an unreal state. One tends to go through daily activities in a mechanical, robot-like manner, without feeling or facial expression. Denial is also common in the early stage of grief. The child who denies the reality of death seems to be saying, "If I don't feel bad, then nothing bad has happened." A third sign of early

* J. Koch, "When Children Meet Death," *Psychology Today* 11 (1977), 64–66, 79–80.

grief is alarm from the sudden realization of danger to oneself. This is reflected in anxiety reactions—deep sighing and rapid breathing. In a child, intense separation anxiety and acute night terrors can also occur at this time.

The second stage of grief—*disorganization*—can involve some or all of the following symptoms: constant weeping, loss of sleep and appetite, a feeling of aloofness from other people, extreme fatigue, irritability, anger, guilt, self-pity, and apathy. Thoughts of the deceased often intrude into consciousness, and there is a yearning and searching for the lost person. The mind wanders and it is difficult to concentrate on school or work. In the final stage—*reorganization*—one integrates the loss and grief and begins to resume interest in work and in other people.

Mourning—the conscious expression of grief—is necessary in order for the bereaved to accept and get over the loss. Unfortunately, it is a human tendency to avoid the pain involved in the mourning process. Such an avoidance of grief has been linked to a variety of psychological disorders later in life, such as depression, psychosomatic problems, and self-destructive behavior.

In mourning, our attention must be consciously directed to memories of the deceased—memories both good and bad. These must be brought up over and over again until desensitization occurs and the emotional ties to the deceased are greatly weakened. The more active the remembering—although it's painful—the shorter the grief period.

It is also necessary for a bereaved person to express his feelings. "Give sorrow words," wrote Shakespeare. "The grief that does not speak/ Whispers the o'er-fraught heart and bids it break." The most important feelings for a child to express are the fear of being abandoned, yearning for the lost figure, and anger at the deceased for dying, or at physicians and others for allowing the death. Emotionally, people seem to need to fight fate for a time and try to recover the lost person and the happy experiences that are lost. Guilt feelings for things that were said or not said to the deceased also need to be ventilated.

CHILDREN AND MOURNING

Children as young as three and four seem able to mourn the
loss of a loved one. However, it is hard for young children to
mourn since it is difficult for them to tolerate intense sadness or
anger. So they tend initially to deny and avoid experiencing the
loss. They need to be repeatedly confronted with the reality and
finality of the death so they can acknowledge the sadness (second
stage of grief). Children need to experience their grief in small
doses: so they will cry for a while and then they will want to
play. They have a short "sadness span." Finally, they need to
accept the loss and form new emotional attachments (final stage
of grief). The process of grieving takes a long time—perhaps a
year or two.

Typically, children do not begin to show grief until they
feel assured that their needs for care and protection will be taken
care of. Verbally inhibited, children express their grief in a variety
of nonverbal ways, including sleeplessness, nightmares, clinging
behavior, and school difficulties. The child may become fearful
that the other parent will die. Children who believe that their
angry thoughts or death wishes caused the death of a parent
need to be reassured that this was not the case, that the death
was not their fault. In moving toward the final "acceptance"
stage of mourning, children may confront their own fears and
wonder aloud why the death occurred, where Mommy or Daddy
is now, and if this death means that another parent or family
member could die also.

Some guidelines for helping children mourn and then let
go of a loved one are:

*Help your children express their thoughts and feel-
ings.*   The best thing a parent can do to help a child cope with
a loss is to assist the child in confronting and accepting the death.
To this end, several approaches can be used.

To help bring grief to the surface, encourage your children
to cry out their grief and talk out their thoughts and feelings for

the deceased. Take the initiative in getting your children to ventilate their grief. At first you may have to verbalize what the child is obviously feeling and let the child know you are feeling it too: "I know you miss Nana very much; I really miss her too."

Children are more likely to speak of their feelings and concerns about death if they can be reassured that whatever they feel, even anger toward the deceased for felt abandonment, is acceptable and normal. The child may indeed feel angry at the deceased for leaving her. Another child may feel guilty, as if she has somehow caused the death of the loved one. Or the child may feel fear and panic at being left alone. The child should be shown that these feelings are natural, and do not negate her love. Once feelings are out in the open, they can be dealt with and finally left behind.

So help your children express their memories, fears, sorrows, regrets, relief, and/or anger and guilt at the passing of a loved one. Any form of expression is beneficial, whether it be through verbalization of feelings or through play or art activities. Don't close off talking about the deceased or pretend that nothing has happened. Silence only teaches children that the subject is taboo; it cannot help them cope with feelings of loss. If children can talk about the loss with a parent, they can manage their feelings.

Reminisce. Help your children polish their memories of the deceased even though this may be painful. Deliberately remember the deceased parent—both the good and the bad—in detail. Grief work is not done all at once; it takes time and remembering.

To promote remembering, try to actively initiate loving, evocative conversations about the loved one who has just died. Refer to past experiences to make it easy for the child to reminisce. You might say, at the dinner table, "Remember how Nana always loved this meat loaf?" Any way you can think of that brings the dead person into the conversation will do. Encourage other family members to openly share their thoughts and feelings about the deceased. A "memory book" with notes and pictures about the person who died can be helpful.

Give honest explanations of death.   Be truthful and open about the facts of death. Remember that children aged six and younger cannot be expected to understand the full meaning of death, especially the finality and universality of it. So gear your explanations to the age of the child.

Talk frequently to the child about the death so he will have to face the reality of it, and so that misconceptions can be cleared up. With younger children, you should make it clear that the physical body cannot function after death. Older children need to be told of the finality of death, that there is absolutely no hope of the deceased returning.

Openly express your love.   In the early stages of mourning, a child needs reassurance that he is loved. This will make him feel more secure. Parents cannot shield their child from painful feelings, but they can help the child to bear them. So openly express your caring—show him in many ways that you love him. One of the best ways to show you care is by your presence; be sure you are really present and available to him with warmth, support, and affection during those difficult months after a traumatic loss. The child needs to feel that he is not alone at this time. Don't forget the importance of a hug or caress.

Don't hide your grief.   It is important for a child to see you express your grief on occasion. Explain to your child that all people cry when they feel sad and that it is O.K.

Philosophical and religious outlooks can help.   You might explain to a child that real love does not die when a loved one dies. The spirit of someone you love does not die. It lives in your heart and your memory. It belongs to you always, and is your treasure.

Also, studies show that if a family is religious and has a transcendental value system, it can enable family members to cope better with the loss and death. Talking about your belief in a deity and an afterlife can comfort children and help them accept death. Loss can become more bearable when you believe that one day you will rejoin the loved one.

SHOULD CHILDREN ATTEND FUNERALS?

Funerals serve the valuable function of allowing the living to acknowledge, accept, and cope with the loss of a loved one. The funeral ritual itself can be used positively to afford a child a sense of closure, to share a sense of loss with other mourners, and to face the reality of death. After viewing the corpse, it's hard to deny the loss. Children may need to touch the corpse to know that their mother or father has truly died, especially after a sudden death. Funerals also serve the purpose of allowing the child to share grief feelings with others who are mourning and to be comforted by them.

Whether or not a particular child should attend depends on the child and the situation. If the child is old enough to understand and wants to participate, being present can help make death less mysterious and frightening. If the child is too immature and/or the adults present are apt to be out of control, it would probably be best to keep the child home with an adult the child trusts, who can answer questions.

A preschool child may be confused and frightened if some adults present are expressing uncontrollable grief. So unless a preschooler is particularly mature, it may be best to keep the child home during the funeral. Many children report that they find wakes distasteful and are angered at being forced to go through the experience. After seeing an open casket, some young children have nightmares of dead bodies or fears about going to sleep for some time after. So parents must decide carefully whether their preschool children should attend a wake or funeral, and if so, for how long. If they feel their children will be psychologically harmed, or if the children oppose attending, they should support their children's needs and wishes.

Experience indicates that children over five are usually sufficiently mature to attend a funeral if they wish. Kept from the funeral of a loved one, they are apt to feel left out. They may think themselves deprived of an opportunity to share their feelings and understand the reality of death.

Prior to attending a funeral for the first time, the child should be prepared for the experience. A parent should fully explain why the funeral is being held, and describe as completely as possible what will take place. The child should know just what is going to happen, how the corpse will be displayed, what will be expected of him, and how people are likely to act (including the possibility of hysterical weeping). He should then be given the option of attending or not, as well as the opportunity to refrain from any part of the ritual that may be distressing, such as viewing the casket. Whatever the child's wishes may be, they should be recognized, discussed, and valued.

The following is the way one parent described a funeral to her seven-year-old to help him decide whether or not to attend the funeral of a loved one:

"A funeral is the way we say goodbye to those we love. Very often we do not have an opportunity to say goodbye and to tell someone of our love for them before death. That is the purpose of a funeral. It is a way for many people who share love and grief for the death of a person to come together. It is an opportunity for many people to say together that we miss a loved one, that we love him and that we will always remember him. Many people find funerals a good way to say goodbye, but some people find them much too sad. Some people like to say goodbye in a different way, perhaps alone and away from others. However, others like the feeling of many people in a group sharing similar feelings. It is your decision whether you will attend the funeral. If you prefer not to, we respect that decision. If you do attend, your mother and I will be with you and will help to explain what is happening and to help you feel as comfortable as possible. Whatever you decide, we know that your love and your feelings for your grandfather are very real to you and that you will miss him as much as we miss him."*

A young child's attendance at the funeral will be a good experience only if a familiar adult accompanies her, to share the occasion and offer information and support as needed. It may be necessary to literally hold the child's hand throughout. The supporting adult must be in control of her own emotions and be able to stay in touch with the child's feelings.

---

* M. D. Glicksen. *Journal of Marriage and Family Counseling* 4 (1978), 79.

WHEN A CHILD'S PET DIES

For many children, the grief they experience over the loss of a pet is the same in quality and intensity as grief that occurs when they lose people they love. This is particularly true for children who have formed a close emotional attachment to the pet. The stages of grief are the same as for a human loss. First there is shock and numbness, during which period the child has difficulty accepting the fact that the pet is dead. The second stage involves internal feelings of unhappiness. During this stage, the child may lash out in anger at the vet or even at themselves for failing to save the pet. The final stage, of resolution and reorganization, is reached when the child has accepted the loss of the pet. At this stage, the child may say, "It would be nice to have a cat again." Some children can go through these stages in just a week. However, if the child-pet bond was really close and long-standing, it will probably take eight to ten months, which is about the same amount of time it takes when a human loved one dies.

WHAT PARENTS CAN DO TO HELP

First, take the loss seriously. Respect the child's grief reaction. Don't treat the loss lightly by saying, "It's just an animal," or "You can always get another cat." Another cat can never replace the uniqueness of the lost animal. So it is important to recognize what the pet meant to the child. Don't suggest to a child that it is weak or foolish to repeatedly cry and talk about the deceased animal. Let the child cry and talk out her grief. Suggest some sort of funeral service and encourage the child to handle the body and bury the pet.

Finally, never rush in with a new pet. Give the child a chance to mourn. This is a valuable experience, which will help the child understand death and prepare her for later losses in life. Recognize that it often takes weeks, even months, before children feel ready to share their life with another pet. Remember that the new pet is not a replacement, but a whole new relationship, a new friend in life, with its own personality.

For additional reading on this topic, I recommend the book *Pet Loss: A Thoughtful Guide for Adults and Children* by Herbert Nieberg and Arlene Fischer (Harper & Row, 1982).

NATURAL AND
MAN-MADE DISASTERS

Natural disasters include such catastrophic events as fires, earthquakes, floods, and hurricanes. Man-made disasters encompass car accidents, nuclear explosions, kidnappings, and so on. Disasters usually occur in a sudden and unexpected way and result in damage to life and/or property. Statistics reveal that each year about a dozen natural disasters of major proportions, and as many as forty of smaller magnitude, occur. These disasters, which arise out of the destructive forces of nature, often in combination with human activities, can leave lasting physical and psychological scars on children who survive them.

The first concern of everyone in a disaster is with physical safety. This is as it should be. However, studies show that after a disaster, parents tend to deny or overlook the harmful psychological effects on their children. Instead, what is needed is crisis intervention whereby the parents try to identify and relieve the stress reactions in a child and reestablish normal functioning as soon as possible.

THE DISASTER SYNDROME

Most people show some signs of emotional disturbance as an immediate reaction to a disaster. These tend to appear in characteristic stages of response. In the first stage, one tends to be stunned and bewildered. Attention is noticeably restricted, behavior tends to be reflexive and automatic, and a lack of feeling is reported (although physiological concomitants of fear are evident).

During the period of recoil, which begins when the initial

stresses have ceased or when the individual has escaped them, the person gradually experiences the total impact of the tragedy. Survivors will characteristically show a childlike attitude of dependency, a need to be with others, and a desire to ventilate their feelings. During this post-traumatic period, common symptoms in children are:

- *Fears and anxieties.* There is often continuing anxiety about recurrence of the disaster, injury, death, separation, and loss.
- *Sleep disturbances.* These include resistance to bedtime, refusal to sleep alone, and recurrent nightmares.
- *School avoidance.* The major reason for not wanting to go to school is fear of being separated from and losing loved ones.

Just as a disaster may vary in nature and severity, children vary in their susceptibility and reaction to such events. Children who have been adequately prepared, and whose parents cope well with the calamity, experience less severe and usually temporary reactions. Relief from the stress, together with the passage of time, will restore equilibrium and appropriate behavior for most children. Understanding and support by parents can speed recovery and, in many cases, prevent serious problems later.

With children, the worst effects of disaster occur when there is actual loss of parents, when the parents themselves have major (often preexisting) psychological problems, or when there are other anxiety-creating factors in their backgrounds (e.g., child abuse or parental alcoholism). Most children show only temporary symptoms, but a minority will exhibit long-term reactions of a severe nature. At least 10 to 20 percent of children who have experienced a trauma will need post-disaster mental health services, to counter chronic anxiety, disorientation, depression, personality changes, etc.

WHAT CAN PARENTS DO TO HELP THEIR CHILDREN?

When a disaster strikes a child, parents should provide "psychological first aid" to alleviate psychic distress and to prevent the development of long-term emotional problems.

Some fundamentals of psychological first aid are:

- It is important for parents and children to acknowledge that something disastrous has happened. To adapt to the experience, victims must deal effectively with the reality. So give the children accurate information about what happened and why. Children are most fearful when they do not understand what's happening around them. Share what you know about the truth of the disaster and its likely impact on the family. The children will want to know when their lives will return to normal. Be honest about this and avoid false assurances. In many instances, the victim's world will never be the same and statements to the contrary will instill false hope. So give an accurate appraisal of the situation.

- Listen and provide a ready ear so as to encourage the verbal expression of feelings associated with the disaster experience. It is important to be able to share one's anger and fears with others who show interest and concern. It has been found that the intensity and duration of children's symptoms decrease more rapidly when their parents are able to communicate understanding of their feelings.

- It is of great importance for the family to remain together during and after a crisis. A family is a child's main source of security. During times of stress, children particularly need this sense of belonging to and being protected by the family. So don't leave your children with a neighbor or relative immediately after a crisis, while you go to inspect the damage. Keep all your children close to you for some time to alleviate their fears of being abandoned and unprotected. According to Anna Freud, the noted child psychoanalyst: "Love for the parents is so great that it is a far greater shock for a child to be suddenly separated from his mother than to have a house collapse on top of him."

- Be comforting and reassuring. You might say, for example, "We are all together and nothing has happened to us," or "We're going to stay real close to you now and take good care of you." Physically hold your child and spend more time with him. By exhibiting courage and calmness, be a pillar of strength that your child can lean on. If you express a continuing fear that the disaster will reoccur, your child will find it very difficult to overcome his own fear.

- Encourage the child to participate in simple, useful tasks as soon as possible. For example, you might ask a child to help clean up the home after a flood. It is comforting to a child to see things being put back in order and family routines being reestablished.

- Refer a child who shows grossly abnormal, violent, or self-destructive behavior to mental health professionals.

Other ways to counteract the effects of a disaster on children are:

Reminisce.   Remembering helps children mourn lost objects. So, for instance, make an effort to assist your children in recalling the burned-down house, its contents, the good and troubled times that were had there.

Cultivate a positive outlook.   Try to think of a disaster as an opportunity as well. If your house was burned down, you can take this occasion to find an even better new house. Think about how you can use this crisis as an opportunity for a better future.

Help them play it out.   Children's play following disasters tends to recreate the experience. Paints, clay, dolls, and water play allow children outlets for pent-up feelings they find it difficult to express verbally.

DIVORCE

The United States has the highest divorce rate among Western nations. In 1982, divorces in this country reached an all-time high of 1.2 million. A recent study revealed that there were 20 million American children under eighteen whose parents were separated or divorced.

Parents in the process of divorce are often in a state of confusion and emotional upheaval. Talking to their children about the divorce has a low priority, since they tend to be angry, depressed, or afraid about the separation. Typically, parents give children no advance warning of a divorce. A parent simply disappears before the children are told anything. Many parents mistakenly assume that their children don't know what's happening or that anything is wrong. Children are extremely sensitive to their parents' feelings, but often don't say anything because they are afraid that if they do they will make matters worse.

The importance of preparing the children for the separation cannot be overemphasized. The physical leaving by one parent is traumatic for children. When children are properly prepared for the divorce, it can help them cope with what is to come, without the loss of confidence and trust in their parents. There is no "best" way for parents to tell children they are getting a divorce. However, the following are some important guidelines you can follow.

WHEN TO TELL

Before discussing the breakup with your children, make sure that you have made every effort to rescue the marriage and that the decision is irrevocable. If a divorce is clearly imminent, experts have agreed that it is best to tell the children at once. If possible, tell the children while you're still living together as a family.

This will give the children some time to talk to both parents about it and get used to the idea. However, too long a waiting period before the actual separation may prolong the agony and lead to false hopes by the children.

WHAT TO SAY

Children should be informed of the impending separation in an honest, straightforward manner—no lies, no excuses, no false promises. Discuss the separation when you and your spouse are both calm and can be sympathetic to the children's needs. The clearer you are about the situation, the more readily the children will adapt to it. It is best if both parents together tell the children about the decision to divorce. This way the children will receive one story and be less confused. It also lessens the possibility of one partner making the other a culprit. Unfortunately, research indicates, most of the time the task of breaking the news is performed by the mother. It usually is best to tell all the children at the same time. The presence of siblings can cushion the shock and provide a sense of support and family continuity. Remember that you just can't tell the children once and then forget about it. They need weeks to assimilate the information and ask questions.

The following guidelines should help you find the right words for your children:

- Let them know that this is a careful, deliberate decision that has not been made impulsively; that you both have tried to work out your problems.
- Give information in a way that does not blame anyone.
- Children do not need to know the painful personal reasons for the divorce. If children ask such questions, inform them that the answers are personal and private and are just between the parents.
- Reassure the children that they will continue to have two parents even though one may live far away, that

both will continue to love them, that the absent parent will see them as often as possible. Children need to know that when parents divorce each other, they don't divorce their children. Each parent still feels the same way about the children and is interested in their welfare.

- Do your very best to make it completely clear to your children that the divorce is not their fault. It is not occurring because of something they have done. They need to hear this again and again. They also need to know that there is nothing they can do to restore the marriage.

- Explain in detail the changes that will take place. Tell them whom they will live with, where they will live, where the noncustodial parent will live, how visits have been arranged, and how often they will occur. This will help the children understand the divorce and its implications for them.

The following are examples of some ways a parent might begin the discussion of the divorce:

"You know Mommy and Daddy haven't been getting along, don't you? We've been unhappy for so long that we've decided to get a divorce. This means Daddy won't be living here any longer."

"You know we have not been getting along well. We are just not happy together. We don't want to remain as miserable as we have been. We have thought about this for a long time. We have now made an important decision—that we should get a divorce and live apart. You were in no way responsible or to blame for this decision. We will always love you and be your parents and take care of you."

"Mommy and Daddy are not happy living together and we have decided that it is best if we get a divorce and live in different houses. We still love you very much and we'll always be your mommy and daddy."

The following are some possible responses to children's questions:

"Why are you divorcing?"

"We have been considering this for a long time, have made many efforts to solve our problems, and we are now finally convinced that we cannot possibly go on together any longer. We just are unhappy living together."

"How can you leave if you love me?"

"My leaving is not connected with loving you. It's because your mother and I do not get along. I love you as much as ever and I always will."

"What can I tell my friends?"

"You can say that your parents have decided to get a divorce and live apart. If you're not comfortable with that, you can always say you'd rather not talk about it."

AFTER YOU TELL

To ease the adjustment for your children, keep in mind the following guidelines:

- Encourage them to ask questions, and listen to their concerns. Remember that telling children once is usually not enough. Establish a dialogue in which the children's questions can be answered, important information repeated, and the children reassured. Repeated conversations give children the chance to digest the painful news and accept the reality of it.

- Specifically ask the children what their reactions are to the divorce. Ask them to identify their feelings for themselves and then to verbalize them. Allow them to express negative feelings. Don't insist that things will be fine, since things are likely to be different and difficult for a while. Don't say, "Be brave. Show us how strong you are." Tears can release painful emotions. So don't let your children bottle up their emotions or try to minimize the loss.

- Do your best to discourage children's wishful thinking

that this will all blow over and that soon they will have
both parents together again in a happy home.

THE EFFECTS OF DIVORCE ON CHILDREN

Though divorce has become an everyday event in American life,
it is extraordinary how ignorant many of us are of its painful
consequences. Divorce is not a one-time event—its effects
linger on.

The most difficult time for all occurs typically during the
first year or two that follow separation; by the end of the second
year of the divorce, most families are regaining balance and
resolving major difficulties.

A study by Judith Wallerstein and Joan Kelly of 131 children
of divorce found that one-third had recovered fully from the
trauma five years after it had taken place. Another one-third
were depressed—the most common symptom of children who
do not cope well. The remaining third fell somewhere in between.
These results support the finding that most divorced parents
view themselves as better off emotionally after a divorce, but
only half of divorced parents see their children as better off.

Researchers have found that young boys generally take longer than young girls to regain emotional balance following separation and divorce. There are some indications, however, that
girls may have delayed reactions, tending toward more difficulties
during adolescence and early adulthood.

AGE-RELATED REACTIONS

Since preschoolers—ages three to five—have limited understanding and ways of coping with problems, they tend to show
the most emotional disturbance after a divorce. Preschool children
are not always able to distinguish between reality and fantasy,
between what they imagine and what actually exists. So preschoolers often experience feelings of guilt, believing that some-

how—possibly because they were bad—they are to blame for the divorce. Preschoolers also tend to fear losing the other parent and being abandoned. Feeling frightened and insecure, they may temporarily regress to immature forms of behavior, such as clinging, whining, nightmares, bed-wetting, temper tantrums, and turning to earlier sources of comfort, such as a stuffed animal.

In regard to school-age children—ages six to twelve—recent research has shown that although they are better able than preschoolers to cope with feelings and fears, their concerns show up in other ways, such as school behavior. Some children become anxious and cannot mobilize the energy and concentration necessary for learning. Others express their anxiety in psychosomatic disorders such as loss of appetite, diarrhea, sleeplessness, and urinary frequency.

EFFECTS ON PARENT-CHILD RELATIONSHIPS

What are some of the effects of the divorce on parent-child interactions?

Typically, custodial mothers become more restrictive and controlling, while noncustodial fathers become more permissive and indulgent but less available. In general, both parents are so preoccupied and upset that they make few maturity demands on the children, communicate with them poorly, are not very affectionate, and maintain inconsistent discipline practices.

In the absence of the spouse, the custodial parent is apt to be less decisive in discipline and to incorporate the children more into the decision-making process. This leads to overly close ties between the custodial parent and the child, with the child treated as friend and confidant.

HOW TO MINIMIZE THE STRESS OF DIVORCE ON CHILDREN

Studies have shown that children of divorce are most apt to adjust well if there is:

- Low interparent conflict and hostility preceding and following the divorce.
- Minimal depletion of financial resources.
- Approval and love from both parents.
- High agreement between parents on child rearing and discipline.
- Authoritative discipline from the custodial parent.
- Cordial and supportive relations between ex-spouses and regular visiting by the noncustodial parent.
- An emotional climate that facilitates the children's discussing divorce-related concerns.
- A good adjustment by the custodial parent to the divorce.

HOW TO RELATE TO AN EX-SPOUSE

Often divorce does not end the bitterness of a poor marriage. Ongoing discord may drain the family's emotional resources and leave the children feeling guilty, angry, and alone. Perhaps the hardest task for the divorced parents is to subordinate their mutual antagonism to the children's needs.

Do your best not to take out on the children any hostility you feel toward your ex-spouse. Don't try to turn the children against the absent parent. Don't make the children feel that they must take sides with you against your former spouse. For their own self-esteem and adjustment, children must love and admire both their parents. Whatever kind of person your ex-spouse is, it is important for your children to make up their own minds about the parent. If you harbor anger toward your ex-spouse, express it to your friends and relatives, not to your children. Since children need the love of both parents, help them to maintain a close relationship with the absent parent through regular and sensible visiting plans. For the sake of the children, former spouses need to be flexible, cooperative, and supportive of each other as parents.

RECOMMENDED READINGS ON DIVORCE

For Children

Terry Berger. *How Does It Feel When Your Parents Get Divorced?* New York: Julian Messner, 1977.

Richard Gardner. *The Boys' and Girls' Book About Divorce.* New York: Science House, 1971.

Margaret S. Pursell. *A Look at Divorce.* Minneapolis: Lerner, 1976.

Janet Sinberg. *Divorce Is a Grown Up Problem.* New York: Avon Books, 1978.

For Adults

Edith Atkins and Estelle Rubin. *Part-Time Father.* New York: Vanguard, 1976.

Leroy G. Baruth. *A Single Parent's Survival Guide: How to Raise the Children.* Dubuque, Iowa: Kendall/Hunt, 1979.

Joanne Bernstein, ed. *Books to Help Children Cope with Separation and Loss.* New York: Bowker, 1977.

Miriam Galper. *Co-Parenting: Sharing Your Child Equally.* Philadelphia: Running Press, 1978.

Susan Gettleman and Janet Markowitz. *The Courage to Divorce.* New York: Simon & Schuster, 1974.

Morton Hunt and Bernice Hunt. *The Divorce Experience.* New York: New American Library, 1979.

Mel Krantzler. *Creative Divorce.* New York: M. Evans, 1973.

James A. Levine. *Who Will Raise the Children? New Options for Fathers (Mothers).* Philadelphia: Lippincott, 1976.

Cathy Napolitane and Victoria Pellegrino. *Living and Loving After Divorce.* New York: Rawson Associates, 1977.

National Institute of Mental Health. *Step-Parenting,* by Renato Espinoza and Yvonne Newman. DHEW Pub. No. (ADM) 78-579, 1979. National Institute of Mental Health, Public Inquiries, 5600 Fishers Lane, Rockville, Md. 20857.

————. *Yours, Mine, and Ours: Tips for Stepparents,* by Sharon Duffin. DHEW Pub. No. (ADM) 78-676, 1978. National Institute of Mental Health, Public Inquiries, 5600 Fishers Lane, Rockville, Md. 20857.

Suzanne Ramos. *The Complete Book of Child Custody.* New York: Putnam, 1979.

Mel Roman and William Haddad. *The Disposable Parent: The Case for Joint Custody.* New York: Holt, Rinehart & Winston, 1978.

Morris Shepard and Gerald Goldman. *Divorced Dads.* Radnor, Pa.: Chilton, 1979.

Ira Victor and Win Anne Windler. *Fathers and Custody.* New York: Hawthorn, 1977.

Judith Wallerstein and Joan Kelly. *Surviving the Breakup: How Children and Parents Cope with Divorce.* New York: Basic Books, 1980.

Robert S. Weiss. *Going It Alone: The Family Life and Social Situation of the Single Parent.* New York: Basic Books, 1979.

———. *Marital Separation.* New York: Basic Books, 1975.

Michael Wheeler. *Divided Children: A Legal Guide for Divorcing Parents.* New York: Norton, 1980.

Persia Wooley. *The Custody Handbook.* New York: Summit Books, 1979.

Periodicals

The Single Parent. Parents Without Partners, Inc., 7910 Woodmont Ave., Washington, D.C. 20014.

Journal Articles

Teresa Levitin, ed. "Children of Divorce," special issue of *Journal of Social Issues,* vol. 35, no. 4, 1979.

Judith Wallerstein. "Children and Divorce," *Pediatrics in Review* 1, no. 7 (January 1980).

REMARRIAGE AND STEPPARENTING

The latest federal census figures indicate that one of two marriages end in divorce and two-thirds of the divorced population marry again within three years. It is little wonder, then, that there are more than fifteen million children under age eighteen living in stepfamilies, as each year, nationally, 500,000 adults become stepparents.

According to Claire Berman, "The word 'step' derives from an Old English term meaning 'bereaved' or 'deprived.' In the past, a man or woman remarried following the death of a spouse; the stepparent was considered a replacement parent, someone who 'stepped in' to rescue a bereaved family." *

CHILDREN'S REACTIONS TO REMARRIAGE

A paramount fear among children involved in remarriages is the imminent loss of the unusually close bond that often develops between child and parent in a single-parent home. They wonder if they will be loved as much after the remarriage. They also dread the thought that another child may be born, who could supplant them. Furthermore, a remarriage often darkens children's hopes for a parental reconciliation. For some children a conflict of loyalties ensues—they may feel they're betraying the still-single parent if they like the new partner of the remarrying one. In addition, they have to make room in their emotional lives for another person—not an easy task for anyone.

Preteens and adolescents are generally less willing to accept

* Claire Berman, *Stepfamilies—A Growing Reality*, Public Affairs Pamphlet No. 609. Copyright © 1982 by the Public Affairs Committee, Inc. Used with permission.

the stepparent, regardless of the adult's efforts and attributes. Experts agree that children under three and near-adult children are the ones who are most accepting of a new parent.

HOW TO TALK ABOUT YOUR INTENTION TO DATE AGAIN

If your former spouse has died, you could prepare the children for your dating by saying something like: "I know you miss your father as I do and you may find it hard to accept my dating again. But we must continue to live our lives as your father would have wanted us to do. It is important for me to date now so I might find someone I will like enough to marry. I'll always love you as much as I do now."

If you and your former spouse are divorced, you could discuss your desire to date again by saying: "Since your father and I will never remarry, I plan to start going out with other men. You may not like this and I can understand it if you don't. I love you very much and I always will."

Don't expect the first meeting between the children and a prospective stepparent to go well. Allow the children time to develop the relationship and don't expect immediate acceptance.

PREPARING CHILDREN FOR A REMARRIAGE

Studies of remarriages involving children show that things work out better when the children have been prepared. Unfortunately, the fear that the child will indeed react in a negative way frequently leads the remarrying parent into making the mistake of leaving the announcement to the last moment or even waiting until the marriage has actually taken place. This leaves children ill-prepared for the adjustment they must make.

Give the children every opportunity to get to know the new lover. Children need to get used to the idea *slowly*. Try and arrange for your children and the new person to spend some time together, both with and without you.

Don't leave the final decision about your remarrying to your children. The children can be allowed to give their opinion, but the determination to remarry is your responsibility. Once you have made the decision, you should tell your children of your intention as soon as possible.

ADJUSTING TO THE REMARRIAGE

After remarriage, unnecessary added strain can develop when the parent, euphoric about getting married again, is so anxious for the child to feel the same way that the stepparent may even be introduced as "your new mother" or "your new father." This instantly ignites resentment and guilt connected with the biological parent, which can backfire and obstruct the child's behavior. This approach also tells the child to use a relationship term before a relationship has developed. Discuss with your children the role of your new partner. For example, you might say, "He's not asking you to love him. He just wants to have a good relationship with you so that you both like and respect each other." Ask the children what they want to call the stepparent. Be flexible enough to let the name change as the relationship matures.

A really trusting relationship takes several years to develop, according to stepfamily research, and the most successful stepparent-stepchild relationships are those in which the stepparent and the parent view that relationship as one of adult friend to the child. This doesn't mean the stepparent must always refuse the role of disciplinarian, because every household must have rules supported by both parents. Rather, the stepparent needs to take the role of secondary disciplinarian. The primary responsibility for discipline belongs to the biological parent. So the stepparent should take a slow, gentle, flexible disciplinary role. The new stepparent needs to be more concerned with making friends with a stepchild than with controlling him.

SOME SUGGESTIONS FOR A NEW STEPPARENT

- Try to get to know the children of your new partner before the marriage.
- Let the children know that you respect their absent parent and understand how much they love and miss the parent. Make it clear that you do not want to replace this parent.

  You want to be a good friend and share whatever you can with the children. You can't be the natural parent, but you can offer warmth, friendship, and a special relationship.

  A child who rejects a stepparent often feels divided in her loyalties to her biological parent who has left. One way to lessen this conflict for the child is to say clearly and more than once, "I will not try to be your mother because I know you already have [have had, if the parent is deceased] a mother. I am a grownup who can become your friend. I know it will take time for us to get to know each other."

- Don't force stepchildren to call you "Mom" or "Dad" unless they feel comfortable with these terms. Rather, suggest that they call you by your first name.
- Don't force a close relationship before a child is ready. Many stepparents make the mistake of wanting to show deep love for their new children almost immediately. Go *slowly* in forming the relationship.
- Never speak negatively about the child's absent parent.
- Don't try to curry favor by frequently giving stepchildren special treats or material things.
- Be responsive to the times your stepchildren want to talk or play with you.
- Be flexible and don't worry if the first encounters don't go well. Don't reject the children even if they initially reject you, as they probably will.
- Try to read as much as you can about stepparenting. A good book is *How to Win as a Stepfamily,* by Emily and

John Visher (Dembner Books, 1982).

- If a stepchild says to you, "You're not my parent, you can't tell me what to do," you could respond, "It's true I'm not your biological father, but I'm acting as a father to you now and I have a responsibility to enforce the rules. I understand how angry you are about this, but you'll have to do it." Be sure to combine discipline with affection and understanding. It is also important for your spouse to support you when you discipline your stepchildren.

- As an "instant parent" to your stepchildren, try to avoid the common tendencies to be either too critical or too obliging.

- Expect to have ambivalent feelings for your stepchildren—love, anger, jealousy, guilt.

- If you have children of your own, it is almost inevitable that you will love your biological children more than your stepchildren. It is suggested by Claire Berman in *Stepfamilies—A Growing Reality* that it is best to be honest and say to your stepchildren, "I do care more for my children because I have known them longer, just as you have a close and loving relationship with your own brother and sister and with your parent. In time, I hope we will grow closer as we get to know one another."

AN ALCOHOLIC PARENT

It is estimated that in America today, 27 million children have at least one parent who is alcoholic. Because of its nature, alcoholism is as harmful to the children as it is to an alcoholic parent. For this reason, it has been called the "family illness." For their own adjustment, the children in the family must face the realities of their parent's illness. Children must be helped to understand the nature of alcoholism, the effect on them as an alcoholic-family member, and how to cope with the stress.

FACTS ABOUT ALCOHOL ADDICTION

Alcoholism is a disease. It is not a sign of weakness of character or mental illness, but is an illness in itself. It is quite common in our society; about 12 million Americans suffer from it. Like any other drug addiction, it is a form of chemical dependency, and it tends to run in families.

Alcoholics drink too much because they have a metabolic disease that makes their bodies and minds crave alcohol. The cause of alcoholism seems to be a combination of genetic and environmental factors. It can affect people of all ages, including children and the elderly. Denial—refusing to admit that there is anything wrong—is a major symptom of alcoholism.

Alcoholism is progressive in nature; as the alcoholic continues his compulsion to drink, he requires more and more doses of alcohol to get the same high. This has increasingly serious effects. At first there are hangovers and morning-after nausea. Later on come blackouts (loss of memory of what happened during drunken episodes). The "shakes"—delirium tremens (delirium with tremors) or D.T.'s—sometimes accompanied by hallucinations, are the withdrawal symptoms of alcohol addiction. Steady drinking can lead to malnutrition, since the alcoholic often doesn't eat properly.

Unchecked, alcoholism can eventually result in serious illness, including cirrhosis of the liver—a killer. And the steady
assault of alcohol on the brain over many years will finally produce vagueness, loss of short-term memory, and inability to cope
with life in general—a condition popularly known as "wet brain."
It is irreversible.

The only solution to alcoholism is complete abstinence.
Treatment for alcoholism involves detoxification and counseling
at one of the ten thousand rehabilitation centers in the United
States. Many insurance policies now cover the cost of this treatment. Typically, an alcoholic entering treatment will spend about
four weeks in a rehabilitation center, where she will receive
individual counseling, along with group sessions with other patients.

Alcoholics Anonymous works hand in glove with the new
facilities. AA is a group of people who have decided to quit
drinking and are trying to live better lives without it. At meetings,
they talk about their experiences and offer help to new people
who are trying to stay sober. Al-Anon groups help relatives and
friends of alcoholics deal with their related problems, while Alateen helps children of alcoholics.

Rehabilitation does work. Alcoholism is now the most treat-
able of chronic diseases. But the alcoholic has to go and get help.
Also, there is no such thing as an ex-alcoholic. An alcoholic remains an alcoholic until he dies, just as a diabetic remains a
diabetic.

THE FAMILY OF AN ALCOHOLIC

The reactions of family members to the alcoholic parent tend to
go through phases. First they attempt to deny the problem. Eventually it becomes all too obvious to the spouse that the drinking
is excessive, so a variety of home remedies are tried, including
reasoning, pleading, bitter accusations, and moral lectures. The
family also stops having friends over or going to social functions
outside the home. Usually these home remedies do not work. A
"what's the use" stage then sets in, when things seem hopeless.

This is followed by the family attempting to take over some of the responsibilities of the alcoholic parent and gradually excluding him from their lives. A separation or divorce may result as the final phase in some families. In others, the alcoholic enters a rehabilitation program and stops drinking.

The alcoholic family tends to live in social isolation. Embarrassment causes family members to stop inviting people into the home lest the family secret be revealed. Family members also tend to become isolated from each other since the alcoholism is usually not a discussible issue. The families feel trapped—like prisoners of war. In captivity, ordinary people tend to become passive and to identify with their captors.

If the mother is alcoholic, research indicates that there are more behavior and emotional problems exhibited by the children. Another finding is that children of alcoholics consider parental fighting and arguing worse than the drinking that it accompanies.

THE EFFECTS ON CHILDREN

Life in the home of an alcoholic parent tends to be chaotic and unpredictable; it frequently involves parental neglect and even physical abuse of the children. Fear, anger, and shame are everyday emotions for the children. They tend to have fewer friends than their peers from nonalcoholic homes. The children may show pseudomaturity since they may often have to act as a parent to themselves or younger children. But underneath this maturity there are feelings of deprivation, dependency, and resentment. Reality awareness may also be impaired, since the alcoholic parent usually denies the problem. Low self-esteem is common because the children of alcoholics tend to feel that because there is something wrong in their family, there is something wrong with them. Studies indicate that parental drinking is most harmful to children aged six to seven, in early adolescence, and again in later adolescence. Typically these children report the feeling that nobody cares about their situation. Perhaps this is the reason they have been called the "forgotten children."

Apart from psychological problems, children of alcoholics are particularly prone to be problem drinkers. The risk for them is four times higher than for their peers. The more severe the parents' alcoholism, the more likely that genetic factors are involved in the development of alcoholism in the children.

WHAT THE SPOUSE OF THE ALCOHOLIC CAN DO

The following are some ways to lessen the impact of alcoholism on your children.

Stay close.   Strive to keep a close relationship with the children. Don't let your tense, upset, or tired feelings distance you from them. Without a positive relationship with you, the children are prone to delinquency, anxiety, and depression.

Communicate.   Be an effective listener and communicator. This involves encouraging your children to express their feelings—their needs, hopes, and fears. Exploration of feelings helps children grow in self-understanding and closeness to you.

Teach about alcoholism.   Provide some relief through knowledge. Teach the facts about alcohol and alcoholism. Encourage your child to ask questions and give honest, objective answers. Don't let the disease become a family secret that can't be discussed. In particular, teach the concept of *responsible drinking* so the children can avoid becoming alcoholics themselves (40 percent to 60 percent of children of alcoholic parents are prone to this).

Encourage outside interests.   Encourage and support the children's becoming involved in school and community activities.

The children need outlets and chances to develop needed relationships with others in activities outside the home. Such activities can also help the children learn to become competent and independent. They promote a sense of having some power and control over one's life (even though the parent's drinking is out of control).

Urge the children to join Alateen. Family members should become involved in Al-Anon and Alateen. These groups provide interaction and camaraderie with people in similar situations. The members of Alateen are children of alcoholic parents. The basic purpose of Alateen is to help such children appreciate their unique identities. It also explores ways of helping or at least coping with an alcoholic parent.

Don't aid the alcoholic's disease. Don't collude with the alcoholic's pathology—don't protect him from being responsible for his own actions. Don't lie, give excuses, or cover up the alcoholic's behavior to protect him from the outside world. Protection from the consequences of his actions only prolongs the illness. Insist that the alcoholic seek help, and try to become involved as a family in the treatment process. Even if the alcoholic is initially reluctant to seek help, if the treatment is good he will respond. So don't sit back and wait for him to decide on his own—insist that he go!

HOW THE CHILDREN CAN COPE

The following are some dos and don'ts for children living with an alcoholic parent.

Don't lecture, moralize, scold, praise, blame, threaten, or argue with your alcoholic parent. This only makes the situation worse. Adults resent children trying to tell them how to run their lives.

Don't pour the alcohol out of bottles in the home. In effect, you will simply be pouring money away. The alcoholic will find ways to obtain liquor.

Don't blame yourself. Alcohol addiction is a disease. You're not the cause of it. Remember that family members will never be able to change their behaviors enough to lessen the alcoholic's need to drink. Even if the family changes in the way desired by the alcoholic, some other deficiency will be assigned as a cause. So trying very hard to be good will not decrease the alcoholic's need to drink.

Don't feel sad or angry just because an alcoholic parent does. Separate your feelings from those of your parents so that the alcoholism does not ruin your life. You have to form your own identity and live your own life.

Don't feel your situation is unique. Probably for every four or five of your peers, there is one who has or had the same problem.

Do share your feelings with someone you can trust. Talk as openly and honestly as you can—about what has been happening at home and inside you.

Do join Alateen, where you can talk with other youths with the same problem. The idea behind Alateen is that you can't change your parent, but you can learn to cope better yourself.

Do read books and pamphlets to understand more about your parent's alcoholism.

With professional help, the whole family can learn how to confront the alcoholic parent when he is sober. In a nonhostile manner, each family member can take turns reading a list of complaints about the drinking problem. You might say something like: "Dad [Mom], I love you a lot, but I don't like the way you acted last night. You really embarrassed me in front of my friends. I want you to get help for your drinking." The truth is painful, but the alcoholic who denies it must get at it.

OTHER FAMILY CRISES

Apart from the traumas already described, such as divorce and the death of a family member, there are a wide variety of serious crises that could befall a family, including physical or mental illness, parental unemployment or money problems, care of an elderly parent, and accidental homicide. A typical case of accidental homicide involves a child who darts out into the street and is killed by a passing car. Some families are able to handle such crises, while others fall apart under the strain. It is not unusual for the families involved to avoid discussing the crisis situation and to end up avoiding one another.

HOW PARENTS CAN HELP

The following are some guidelines for preventing children from being overwhelmed by a family crisis.

Discuss the crisis with the children. It is only natural for parents to want to protect their children from sad or unpleasant information and experiences. Some parents "keep it a secret" that a baby brother or sister was born dead or severely retarded. Other parents refuse to answer honestly questions about a relative who is seriously ill, or a father who has lost his job. Stoicism and denial is the strategy adopted by many parents, who believe that dwelling on a bad situation only makes it worse.

The evidence, however, indicates that children sense when something is wrong or something is being held from them. This secrecy makes the children feel insecure, confused, and alienated from their parents. So when there is a problem that affects the whole family, it is usually best to bring it out in the open. Families who successfully handle such crises are the ones who communicate among themselves a lot. Tell your children the truth about a crisis so they will be better prepared to cope with it. Be honest and open about the facts. Explain the situation in language the children can understand. End with reassurances that you are there to talk, answer questions, and—above all—support, protect, and love them.

For example, you might explain a father's unemployment by saying, "Daddy just lost his job, so he'll be going out looking for a new job. It's going to be hard on all of us for a while, since we won't have as much money as before and will have to cut down on expenses. But we'll get through it, and you can help a lot by giving up a few things, like sleep-away camp this summer. This is a time for everyone in the family to pull together and help out."

Be comforting and reassuring.   After explaining the facts, be available to comfort and reassure the children. Let them know that the family will adapt and weather the crisis. For example, in talking about parental unemployment, assure the children that there will always be enough money for food and that sooner or later you'll get a new job.

The children will also need a good deal of love and affection at this time. Tell them often just how much you care about them.

Involve the children in decisions.   It is a good idea to have family discussions about how to cope with the crisis situation, discussions in which there is a give-and-take, with all members feeling free to ask questions and contribute to decision-making. Try to get the children actively involved in figuring out ways to cope with the situation so they can gain a sense of mastery, of being in control of the family's fate.

Resolve to grow from the experience.   Be positive in your outlook and try to look for a silver lining. You might say, for example:

"One good thing about this—it's bringing us closer together," or "We can handle this—we're the kind of family that has the strength to do it."

The Chinese symbol for "crisis" is a combination of two other symbols, meaning danger and opportunity. Every family crisis represents a danger to the stability of the family and a severe challenge to all its members. But the same crisis also represents an opportunity for the family to change and grow in closeness and strength of character.

Remember that much of the inner strength that people acquire in life comes from facing up to and overcoming life's problems and misfortunes. By successfully coping with a family crisis, your children can learn some valuable lessons: how much family members mean to one another; the importance of turning to other people; how to problem-solve together; how to really communicate. Most important, they will have gained a sense of mastery. They will learn that they and the family have what it takes to survive. This understanding of their inner resources can help your children move on to a higher level of maturity.

Seek social support. For problem-beset families, an important buffer against stress is social support—turning to other people and to organizations for help. Studies of families facing problems invariably reveal that the ones that sought advice and help from friends, relatives, and community groups were distinctly more successful than those that did not. This is an important lesson for your children to learn.

Respect family privacy. Children need to know that some family crises are private and should not be revealed to other people. You can successfully appeal to older children's sense of privacy and openly discuss with them the reasons why outsiders might misunderstand the issue or be unsympathetic about it. You might say something like: "This is nobody's business but our own. Let's keep it private and not tell anyone. There are people who might not understand about the mental illness of your mother, and we want to make things as easy as possible until things get better."

PART II

CONCERNS OF YOUTH

Many of the concerns of youth are about "sensitive" topics, and parents are often reluctant to talk about them, or feel awkward in discussing them. This is unfortunate, since these are very important issues, about which children and adolescents need more parental guidance, not less.

A major parenting responsibility, then, is to help children comprehend these more complex issues and questions of life, such as conception and death. In a very real sense, knowledge is power—power to anticipate events and to prepare oneself for them. With information about the important topics, children are better able to understand and cope with them. Included in this section are normal concerns of young people about sexuality, love, God and religion, careers, death, war, and other matters.

TALKING ABOUT SEX AND SEX EDUCATION

Many parents today still find it very difficult to talk to their children about sex. It is ironic that after the so-called sexual revolution of the sixties, so many parents in the eighties are as tongue-tied as ever when it comes to discussing sexuality with children. A recent survey of families in Cleveland found that 85 to 95 percent of the parents *never* discussed sex or intercourse with their three-to-eleven-year-old children. Forty percent hadn't discussed menstruation with their daughters.

Children of all ages need to talk about sex and most parents would like to be able to teach their children about it—to be "askable parents," whom children turn to with all their questions. Sex education in schools is only meant to supplement the sex education in the home. Parents should be the primary source of their children's knowledge and values about sexuality. When parents avoid this responsibility, children are apt to receive incorrect information from inappropriate sources.

How should you talk to a child about sex? The cardinal rule is to answer questions honestly, directly, and simply. Don't be vague, evasive, or untruthful. Gear your answers to the child's level of understanding and experience.

You don't have to be an expert to talk to your child about sex. As a parent, you possess a great deal of knowledge about human sexuality. If your child asks a question you don't know, simply say you'll look it up. Being an askable parent is more important than knowing everything.

When should sex education begin at home? As soon as a child is old enough to ask questions, he is old enough for an appropriate answer. This can be as early as two. If your children do not ask questions about sex and reproduction by the age of seven, they have probably received the impression that it is a forbidden topic somehow. This attitude is often conveyed to children without the parent being aware of it. If you feel that your child is way past the age when he should be asking, bring the subject up. Most likely you will discover that he has found out what he wanted to know elsewhere—from his friends, for instance. Be sure to check up on the accuracy of his information, since he is likely to have misperceptions.

GENERAL GUIDELINES

Here is advice drawn from authorities on how to handle sex talks:

Use correct terms.   Teach your child a correct vocabulary for parts and functions of the body. Call a penis a penis rather than using an infantile euphemism such as "wee wee." The following words convey clear meanings: penis, vulva, vagina, testicles, buttocks, anus, breasts, sexual intercourse, clitoris, nipples, semen, erection, ejaculation, masturbation, and condom. These are not too hard for children to say. Use them naturally and freely in talking to your children about sex. The use of correct terms makes the subject less confusing, mysterious, and difficult to discuss.

Take the initiative.   Sensing parental discomfort, school-age children are less likely than preschoolers to ask questions about sex. But they are deeply curious and concerned about the subject. If your children rarely ask questions, look for opportunities to bring up the topic. Take advantage of "teachable moments," occasions when your child is likely to be open to sexual information and guidance. You might remark about something you see in the newspaper or on television. Or you could make an observation about animal behavior, or pregnant relatives. "Diane is developing breasts" is a way to broach the topic of puberty. You might also read with your children some sex books written for their particular age.

Be matter-of-fact.   Treat the question as you would any other question by the child. If children are given facts about sex in a straightforward manner, they will accept them as the matters of fact they are.

Be brief.   Too often parents "overanswer" questions. Don't give a lecture or overwhelm your child with information. A long speech will only turn your child off. Informal, spontaneous exchanges are best. Be brief and leave the door open for further discussion. A good rule of thumb is to give a minimal answer and then wait to see whether your child is satisfied. If she wants more, she will ask.

Remember to answer only the question that's asked. Listen carefully to what your child is asking. If the question's not clear, try to find out the meaning by asking the child, "In what way?" or "What do you mean?" Remember the story of the little boy who asked his father, "Where did I come from?" And then, after listening to a long discourse on reproduction, the child said, "Well, the boy next door came from Chicago. I just wanted to know where I came from."

So give only the information the child requests, and for the most part offer it only when asked. This avoids the common error of telling too much too soon.

Be honest.   Don't let embarrassment distort the truth. Some parents still mislead children by old myths such as the "stork." Research indicates that when children are deprived of honest answers and explanations, they will construct their own explanations and myths. Inventive myth-making often occurs.

For example, today's child is prone to give doctors and hospitals special powers in the process of baby-making.

Also noteworthy is the finding that children are likely to be misled and confused by analogies. They take too literally the metaphor of the father's "planting a seed in the mother." The seed is seen as resulting in plants growing in soil attached to the wall of the mother's stomach, watered occasionally by the father's semen. Eggs are seen as brittle, encased objects produced by hens, geese, and ducks.*

Expect to be uncomfortable.   Most parents feel uncomfortable talking to their children about sex. It's O.K. to feel this way as long as you don't let it paralyze you. Cope with this discomfort by:

- *Starting early.* Begin sex education when your children are very young so you will feel more comfortable and confident discussing it when they are older.
- *Desensitization.* When alone or with your spouse or trusted friend, practice saying the words relating to sex which you find difficult to say, until the words come out naturally. You might also try to rehearse some of your answers in advance.
- *Being open.* Don't be ashamed to admit to your older children that you feel awkward in discussing sex. You might say, "This isn't an easy subject for me to talk about. When I was young it wasn't discussed in the home. But I believe this is an important topic and I want to discuss it with you." Your children will respect you for your honesty.

Examine your attitudes.   If human sexuality arouses in you feelings of guilt, disgust, or shame, you are likely to pass on

* See R. J. Goldman and J. D. Goldman, "How Children Perceive the Origin of Babies and the Roles of Mothers and Fathers, in Procreation: A Cross-National Study," *Child Development* 53 (1982), 491–504.

this attitude to your children. If this is the case, you need to develop more healthy attitudes by readings, courses, or discussions. In the event you are unable to accomplish this, sex education for your children should be offered by providing books, enrolling them in courses, or referring them to a trusted adult who can give them the proper guidance.

The most important aspect of sex education is not providing information; it is conveying values, standards, and attitudes.

Be a good listener.   Children need to feel that their ideas and concerns about sex are worth listening to. Never make fun of any area of a child's ignorance or belief. Let your children know that they can trust you and you'll never use against them anything they reveal to you about their sexuality.

Listen with understanding even if your child expresses values or opinions about sex that differ from your own. Often these are not deeply entrenched ideas or values, but are only part of a sorting-out process that adolescents go through. If you disagree, then clearly state your viewpoint, and why you feel that way. Keep the door open for further discussion of the issue. Don't cut off communication by harsh criticism or condemnation of the child's beliefs.

Be an askable and accepting parent.   That is, encourage open communication so your children will seek you out as an important resource. Get across to your child at an early age that all questions are welcome.

Give immediate feedback.   Be prepared to handle questions as they come up. Don't needlessly postpone your response, since your child is likely to have forgotten what she wanted to know by the time you are ready to discuss it.

Expect to repeat yourself.   Some parents expect sex education to be a one-shot talk about the facts of life. But children need to learn about sex and reproduction many times, since they assimilate information slowly, with much repetition. So be prepared to have the same questions come up over and over again as part of an ongoing dialogue. Give increased elaboration and detail as the child matures. Like religious education, sex education is a continuous process that begins early and continues throughout the life span.

Be discreet about your sex life.   Don't feel obligated to give details of your own sex life to your children. If your child asks if you have intercourse, you might give a general reply: "Yes, adults who love each other usually do." Or if you don't wish to answer, say, "That's personal."

If your child observed you having sexual relations, try to find out what he thought was happening and correct any misconceptions. According to Freud, children may interpret intercourse as an aggressive act, inflicted by the father on the mother, and both parents may sound as if they are in pain. So encourage your child to talk about it in order to learn if he has distorted what he has seen and to help him deal with his reactions. Tell him it's an act of love and affection that gives great pleasure, and that it's done in private. Keep your explanation short and simple.

RECOMMENDED READINGS ON HUMAN SEXUALITY

For Parents

William A. Block. *What Your Child Really Wants to Know About Sex— and Why.* Englewood Cliffs, N.J.: Prentice-Hall, 1972.
Mary Calderone. *The Family Book About Sexuality.* New York: Harper & Row, 1981.
Child Study Association of America. *What to Tell Your Child About Sex.* New York: Pocket Books, 1968.

Sol Gordon. *Let's Make Sex a Household Word.* New York: John Day, 1975.

Marilyn Lyman. *Sex Education at Home—A Guide for Parents.* Planned Parenthood, 1120 E. Genesee Street, Syracuse, N.Y. 13210.

Wardell B. Pomeroy. *Your Child and Sex: A Guide for Parents.* New York: Dell, 1974.

Arlene S. Uslander, Caroline Weiss, and Judith Telman. *Sex Education for Today's Child—A Guide for Modern Parents.* New York: Association Press, 1977.

For Children 6–10

Jennifer Aho and John Petros. *Learning About Sex.* New York: Holt, Rinehart & Winston, 1981.

Sol Gordon. *Girls Are Girls and Boys Are Boys.* New York: John Day, 1974.

Eric Johnson and Corrine Johnson. *Love and Sex and Growing.* New York: Bantam, 1979.

Lennart Nilsson. *How Was I Born?* New York: Delacorte Press (Seymour Lawrence), 1975.

For Children Under 6

Sol Gordon and Judith Gordon. *Did the Sun Shine Before You Were Born?* Syracuse, N.Y.: Ed-U-Press, 760 Ostrom Avenue, 1977.

Sidonie M. Gruenberg. *The Wonderful Story of How You Were Born.* New York: Doubleday, 1970.

Per Holm Knudson. *The True Story of How Babies Are Made.* Chicago: Children's Press, 1973.

Peter Mayle. *Where Did I Come From?* Boston: Lyle Stuart, 1973.

WHERE BABIES
COME FROM

By the time children are in kindergarten, they should know where babies come from and the facts about obvious anatomical differences between boys and girls. The following are some questions commonly asked by preschoolers, and suggestions for answers. Don't use these answers verbatim—find the style that suits you best.

"Where do babies come from?"
> "Babies grow inside their mommies until they are ready to be born."

"Where does a baby grow inside the mommy?"
> "In a special place just for babies, called a uterus."

"How does the baby get out?"
> "From a special opening in the mommy's body for the baby to come through."

"How does a baby get inside the mommy?"
> "A small sperm from a daddy's body enters the mommy's body and meets a tiny egg from the mommy. They join together and the baby grows from that. When it's big enough, the baby is born."

School-age children, aged six to nine, are ready for more detailed information and often are curious about the role of the father.

"How do you have sexual intercourse?"
> "The mommy and daddy lie close together and feel loving toward each other. The father's penis fits into the mother's vagina. That's called sexual intercourse."

"Does the man urinate inside the woman?"

"No. Even though the penis carries the man's urine and semen out of his body, it can't do both at the same time."

"How does the baby get out of the mother?"

"A special hole opens up in her body between her legs. The skin and muscles stretch and there is enough room for the baby to squeeze through, usually with the head coming first. The doctor helps the baby in getting out."

SEX PLAY AND MASTURBATION

Normal curiosity causes children to want to know what the other sex looks like. As a result, they may look at or touch another child's genitals while "playing doctor." Rather than making a big issue of it, you can either direct the children's attention to a substitute activity or say, "Our bodies are private, so we don't play games like that." In this way you set an appropriate limit without making children feel they are "bad" or have done an "evil" act.

MASTURBATION

Many boys enjoy rubbing their penises occasionally. Some girls enjoy rubbing the area near the outside of the vagina or rubbing their breasts. Masturbation is a normal expression of sexuality at any age. In early childhood it is part of the child's exploration of his body; later it becomes a natural release for sexual tension. If a child masturbates in public, you might say, "It's O.K. to touch your penis [vagina/vulva], but it's something you do in private—not in front of other people." Distraction is another effective way to curb public masturbation. Above all, don't say, "It's bad," or that the child will go insane because of it. Masturbation just does not cause insanity, skin blemishes, blindness, poor sexual adjustment in adult life, or any other troubles parents may worry about.

Children should be given privacy to masturbate if they like. Respecting a child's privacy means knocking on a child's bedroom door before entering.

PREPARING A CHILD
FOR PUBERTY

Children need to be prepared for puberty so they won't be frightened or bewildered by the sudden changes in their bodies. So *before* the event occurs, tell your child exactly what to expect, both physically and psychologically, and point out the normality of it. In this way, you will dispel the feeling that it is unexpected or different from what is happening to others. Boys and girls would also like to be told about the changes happening to each other's bodies.

If talking doesn't seem to be effective, books about puberty can be helpful since older children can read them on their own. (See recommended books on pages 107–108.)

WHAT IS PUBERTY?

Basically, puberty consists of the maturation of the gonads: the ovaries in the female and the testes in the male. Triggered by the pituitary gland, these two glands start to secrete sex hormones (androgens in males, estrogens in females) in greater quantity, and begin to produce mature sperm and ova. In addition to these changes, known as primary sex characteristics, the increase in sex hormones causes noticeable changes in the skin, hair, and body shape. The latter are called secondary sex characteristics. Due to the surge in sex hormones, children experience heightened sexual arousal.

Individual differences in growth rates make it impossible to predict exactly when puberty will begin in a child. Because of better health and nutrition, both sexes have been maturing earlier today than in previous generations. For most young girls, puberty changes begin between the ages of nine and twelve (boys usually begin between eleven and fourteen) and continue until the mid-teens.

WHAT GIRLS NEED TO KNOW

Menstruation is a very important and personal part of being a woman. Simply defined, menstruation is the periodic shedding of blood and tissue from the female reproductive organ called the uterus. The term "menarche" refers to the first menstrual period in a girl's life. The menarche is an important event for girls and one that parents should not ignore. To menstruate without preparation can be a frightening experience. A girl may think she is dying or very sick.

By age nine, girls should be learning about menstruation. Don't wait for your child to bring up the subject. In a study conducted by the Project on Human Sexual Development in Cambridge, Massachusetts, it was found that almost 40 percent of the parents of girls aged nine to eleven had never even mentioned menstruation.

In most countries the mean menarcheal age is eleven. Some girls begin to menstruate at nine or ten years of age, while others may not start until they are sixteen or seventeen. Children should be reassured that it is perfectly normal if, among their groups of friends, they are the first or one of the last to begin menstruation.

Also explain that periods often do not occur regularly when they first appear. Missing a period does not mean you are pregnant. During adolescence, it is not unusual for periods to occur once every three, four, five, or six months.

A broadening of the hips is the first sign of puberty. This is followed by increase in breast size, budding of the nipples, and growth of hair in various regions, especially pubic hair in the genital area and hair in the armpits. Voice changes and a gradual coarsening of the skin are also apparent. When these secondary sex characteristics start appearing, you should provide your daughter with sanitary napkins, since the menarche will soon follow.

"What happens when you menstruate?" In response to this question you might say: "Inside your abdomen are two small ovaries. Each is filled with hundreds of tiny undeveloped eggs. Starting at about age eleven, once a month or so, one egg develops and pops out of an ovary. Each ovary is connected to the uterus by a special tube called a fallopian tube. You don't know when the egg—or ovum—comes out of the ovary; you don't feel anything. But about two weeks later, you have your period. This means that since you aren't making a baby and don't need the lining inside the uterus, it can leave your body. This bloody material comes out through the vagina, a special place between your legs. This flow lasts for a few days—usually four or five. Since the flow lasts a period of time, it is often called a 'period.'

"Most girls feel fine during menstruation and can do all the things they usually do. Sanitary napkins are designed to absorb the menstrual flow externally. Another kind of product, called a tampon, is worn inside the vagina and absorbs the flow internally. The napkin or tampon should be changed every four or five hours during the heavy-flow days, to keep odors or stains from forming.

"The menstrual discharge is heaviest during the first few days. The total menstrual discharge amounts to about half a cup, but there's only four to six tablespoons of blood. The rest is made up mostly of extra uterine lining, which explains why the discharge is often brownish in color.

"Women usually menstruate until they are about fifty years old. The end of menstruation, called menopause, occurs between forty-five and fifty-five years."

If menstruation should start when your daughter is in school, advise her to go to the school nurse for assistance. She should also know that the flow is slow enough to allow her to get home if need be or to some other place where she may obtain a sanitary napkin.

Many girls have no menstrual problems at all, but it is not

abnormal for others to experience mild discomfort or minor pain in the lower abdomen or back for the first day or two of their periods. Such cramps seem to be most common between the ages of fifteen and twenty-five, until the process becomes completely regularized. Most cramps are the result of muscle contractions of the uterus as it sheds the lining of unneeded tissue and blood built up to nourish the egg cell had it been fertilized. Moderate exercise releases tension, increases circulation, and can help relieve cramps.

For a brief time prior to the onset of menstruation, some girls may feel somewhat moody, tense, or tired—a condition known as "premenstrual tension." The reason is simple. The female hormones, estrogen and progesterone, that cause the lining of the uterus to thicken usually make one feel especially well. Just before menstruation begins, the production of these hormones is reduced, resulting in a let-down feeling. This feeling is strictly temporary and disappears as mentruation starts.

What should be the emotional reaction of a parent to a girl's menarche? Clearly, it is inappropriate to convey the feeling that it is a sickness and to pass on the tradition of the "curse." In addition, you should avoid the message: "Now you can have a baby." This phrase may have been proper at an earlier time, when girls menstruated later and married earlier. Today, however, this comment is inappropriate for a twelve- or thirteen-year-old female, who is not ready to think about parenthood.

Since research indicates that most girls experience strong ambivalent and even negative emotions about the beginning of menstruation, it does not seem wise to say "Congratulations!" Such a saying is likely to make your child doubt that you understand the complexity of her emotions. The most appropriate response, according to many psychologists, is to simply acknowledge the event with a message which shows you realize that something important has occurred. Thus you might say, "Something special has happened!" Couple this with a hug or a kiss, and a gift of flowers or a charm for a charm bracelet.

WHAT BOYS NEED TO KNOW

When most boys are twelve to fourteen years of age, their scrotum and testicles begin to enlarge and after this the penis increases in size. They also have a growth of pubic hair, followed by a growth of hair in the armpits, on the chest, and then the face. Their voices deepen, their shoulders broaden, and they grow taller and heavier.

About one year after the beginning of these changes, they usually have acquired the capacity to produce and ejaculate sperm, and they may have nocturnal emissions ("wet dreams"). During sleep, there may be a discharge of semen, a white, sticky fluid which contains the sperm. A boy may or may not have a sex dream along with the emission. Frequent erections (stiffening of the penis), and sexual thoughts and desires, will also appear.

Boys should be reassured that wet dreams are normal and that they shouldn't worry about getting their pajamas or sheets messy. Also, it is normal for some boys to develop later than others. The late developers often feel uncomfortable because their penis and scrotum are smaller than the other boys'. Early-developing boys will show puberty changes as early as ten or eleven.

RECOMMENDED PAMPHLETS ABOUT PUBERTY WRITTEN FOR CHILDREN

For Girls

About Menstruation. Planned Parenthood of America, 810 Seventh Avenue, New York, N.Y. 10019.
Having Your Period: Do You Know the Facts About Menstruation? Planned Parenthood of America, 810 Seventh Avenue, New York, N.Y. 10019.
Why Girls Menstruate. American Medical Association, 535 N. Dearborn Street, Chicago, Ill. 60610.

For Boys

For Boys: A Book about Girls. Personal Products, Milltown, N.J. 06850.

For Both Sexes

Changes: Sex and You. Department of Health and Human Services, Pub.
#HSA 80-5648.

Growing Up: Specially for Preteens and Young Teens. Planned Parenthood
Center of Syracuse, 1120 E. Genessee Street, Syracuse, N.Y. 13210.

HOMOSEXUALITY

Be prepared to discuss the meaning of homosexuality with your children. A homosexual is a person who in his or her adult life consistently prefers to develop emotional and sexual relationships with people of the same sex. We really don't know why some people become homosexuals as adults.

Homosexuality is not a choice that people make, but is a fundamental fact about their personalities. Although gains have been made in reducing the stigma associated with homosexuality, most people in our society still do not accept homosexuals and homosexual acts.

It is estimated that about 5 percent of the adult population of the United States is homosexual. On the other hand, a Kinsey study over a decade ago revealed that about 60 percent of American men and 30 percent of American women have had at least one overt, intentional homosexual experience by the age of fifteen. So be sure your children understand that an isolated homosexual experience is not a sign of a fixed sexual preference.

PORNOGRAPHY

Children today are exposed to a steady stream of sexually explicit pictures in magazines and books, as well as on television and motion picture screens. They will undoubtedly see not only crude pictures of completely naked persons but also scenes depicting a variety of deviant sex acts such as sadomasochistic scenes. It is virtually impossible for them to avoid even hard-core pornography, since it is as close as the local newsstand. The porn business is thriving and in 1981 it was estimated to have grossed $6 billion, almost as much money as the conventional movie and record industries combined.

We must first of all realize that pornography can be harmful to our children. Much of it now portrays sexual violence, degradation, and humiliation rather than just nudity. Common themes include sadism, incest, child molestation, rape, and even murder. Pornography can affect childrens' attitude to sex in two ways. First, it depersonalizes sex and reduces it to a mechanistic function devoid of any feelings. It shows sex without dignity, respect, and love. It glorifies hedonism and self-centeredness rather than love, tenderness, and commitment. Secondly, it suggests that there is nothing out of the ordinary about sexually brutalizing other people, especially women and children. Aggressive sex is portrayed as normal and exciting. Consequently, it does not seem to be a coincidence that the last ten years have been marked by a rise in both pornography sales and crimes of sexual violence.

Many parents ask, "But what can I do?" The best approach is a middle ground between blind and unproductive censorship on one hand and completely ignoring the problem on the other. Parents need to express to their children their firm convictions about pornography. Let your children know from an early age— perhaps nine or ten—your opinions about pornography and the reasons underlying your judgments. Take notice of what your children are exposed to, and then talk with them about the magazines, movies, and television shows that come their way. You can short-circuit pornography's potentially destructive impact by discussing it in a straightforward way before the images overwhelm your children's minds. If members of your family buy pornographic books or magazines, tell them you want the material out of your home.

THE MEANING OF LOVE

. . . how many who love never come any nearer than to
behold each other as in a mirror; seem to know and yet
never know the inward life; never enter the other soul; and
part at last with but the vaguest notion of the unwise, on the
borders of which they have been hovering for years?
—GEORGE MACDONALD, *Phantastes*

Romantic love is to a great deg. ɛe narcissistic—a form of self-love in which one lover sees himself in the other, and concludes they are soul mates. It tends to be an encapsulating, monopolizing love that becomes obsessive, shuts out the world, and quickly burns itself out. In contrast, mature love is a generous, outgoing kind of love that is expansive—it enables you to love yourself and other people more. When you have mature love you want to reach out and embrace the whole world. A constructive energy and generosity of the spirit is released by this kind of love, which can go on forever.

"Love," in most of its meanings, involves concern for the other person's welfare and feelings. According to the philosopher Martin Buber, "Love is not the enjoyment of a wonderful emotion, nor even the ecstasy of a Tristan and Isolde, but the responsibility of an I for a Thou." So mature love is quite different from infatuation and the feeling of being in love. Mature love is placing the other person's welfare on a par with one's own.

Mature love perceives the lover clearly and penetratingly—faults and all. It is nonpossessive, fosters individuality in the loved one, and can be enjoyed throughout the life span. Our society does not value mature love very highly—the type of love which involves commitment, empathic understanding, companionship, acceptance, trust, comfort, and psychological intimacy. Mature love is a rare treasure that one has to keep working at to maintain.

Self-esteem and self-confidence are essential prerequisites

for true love. Love's aim is a kind of unfolding of oneself and another through an intimate relationship. Love fosters the uniqueness of both partners and encourages continual self-actualization in each person. Thus you have to love yourself before you can really love another. If we do not love ourselves, it is almost impossible to believe that another can love us, so it is hard to accept love. Loving oneself means a genuine interest, caring, and respect for oneself—not a narcissistic obsession with oneself.

Parents should talk to their children from an early age in order to sensitize them to other people who cannot really love. The latter individuals cannot trust; some are exploitative, some simply have difficulty in interacting with in-depth intimacy. Some resent obligation and try to avoid long-term commitments. Others just cannot let a loved one grow in an atmosphere free of jealousy and possessiveness.

According to Leo Buscaglia, Professor of Education at the University of Southern California, to truly love another is life's greatest challenge. It requires more understanding, acceptance, tolerance, knowledge, and strength than any other human endeavor.

GOD AND RELIGION

Since the earliest days of mankind, people have felt a great innate need to know and worship God. Consequently, religion has been a major force—usually good—throughout history.

Many parents have problems communicating with their children about religion these days, when there is a crisis of belief in many denominations, when moral values are changing and old orders are questioned. For most parents, religiously based moral convictions and codes of right and wrong still form the basis for the decisions they make and the values and standards they try to teach their children.

What value does religion have for children? First of all, it satisfies the universal human impulse to find something to believe in, something that gives meaning to life and death. A few years ago, the sociology department of Duke University did a study on "peace of mind." One of the factors they found most likely to contribute to emotional and mental stability was "finding something bigger than yourself in which to believe." Religion gives a child the feeling that there is someone "in charge" of the world.

Religion also offers young people guidance as to moral values, as well as consolation and comfort in adversity. It can make children feel less selfish, and more aware that they are part of a large circle, and not the center. Another important aspect of religion is that it teaches a child that she is loved, and is of inestimable worth. It bolsters a child's self-esteem and promotes a reverence for life. Finally, religion advocates the brotherhood of man and love for all men.

So whatever their particular religious beliefs, most parents want to encourage their children to believe in something, whether they call it God or simply goodness. What you explain will, of course, depend on your own religion. But the following are some guidelines on when and how to introduce religious ideas so that your children will best understand them. To prevent confusion in children, there are two significant factors for parents to consider in teaching religious concepts: the age of the child and the manner in which you teach.

EFFECTIVE METHODS FOR TEACHING RELIGION

Perhaps the best method for teaching children about religion is by your daily devotion to it despite difficulties that test your faith. It will be hard for your children to take religion seriously when you practice only one day of the week. Be sure to tell your children of the sustenance you have found from your own religious experiences.

Apart from your example, you should talk about God with your children on a regular basis and let them know that you welcome their questions. Don't hesitate to convey your religious convictions to your children and to discuss your understanding of God—and the moral values by which you live.

If parents have sharp religious differences, they should make every effort to leave the child out of their arguments, and to come to a compromise which leaves the least tension between themselves.

AGE-APPROPRIATE INSTRUCTION

When you talk to your children about God, choosing explanations appropriate to their age will help you enlighten rather than confuse them.

Young children. Because preschool and early elementary school children think in concrete terms, comprehending the abstract nature of God poses problems for them.

Regardless of their families' religious affiliations, children

envision God as a bearded, grandfatherly individual who lives
in the sky, a sort of Santa Claus minus the red suit.

Young children need to know that God is a very big idea
which is hard to understand all at once and that they will want
to learn more about it and talk about it many times. Gradually,
you can help them realize how difficult it is for man, the finite,
to comprehend God, the infinite.

Young children are naturally faith-filled people to begin with
and will accept their parents' beliefs about God and moral issues.
Just as youngsters trust and have faith in their parents, they will
have faith in God. They will have feelings of love, of awe, of
trust, of fear, in somewhat the same proportions as they have
these feelings for their parents. With young children we should
emphasize the magnitude of God's love and forgiveness, rather
than the fearful aspects of religion.

It is also wise to be prepared for their questions. When
young children ask questions, it is important to satisfy their curiosity while not giving them more information than they can
assimilate. But don't give misleading or inaccurate answers. If
you don't know the answer to a factual question, look it up in
the Bible or a reference book, or just admit that many things are
still a mystery to us all. You can respond best to your child's
questions if you have clarified your own beliefs as much as possible. A befuddled parent has little to offer a confused child.
Preparing some appropriate responses to children's most common questions can help you answer your child clearly.

The following are some possible answers to the common
questions of young children.

"Why can't I see God?"

"God is a spirit, like the wind. We cannot see the wind, but
we can see the work of the wind—trees sway, leaves rustle,
and we feel it rush by. We cannot see God since He has no
body, but when we see people showing love or kindness
to each other, we know God is there."

"We cannot see God, only his creations."

"God is love. You know I love you but you can't see my love as you can see my face. God, like my love, is real and good, but you can't see or touch God."

"God is like the life force in a seed. You cannot see it if you cut the seed open, yet it is there and its power is tremendous."

"Where is heaven?"

"We don't know where heaven is. Some say it's in the sky."

"We do not know for certain. Since God is not a person, he does not live in a place like we do."

"When is God present?"

"When there is love, or mercy, or kindness, then there is God."

"What is a sin?"

"Sin means doing something wrong."

"Why is there evil in the world?"

"God has given us free will to choose good or evil, and while we are strengthened when we choose good, some people don't."

"Why are there different religions?"

"Since people have different ideas of what God is like, they have created different ways to talk about Him and worship Him."

"How can an all-loving God allow poverty, disease, and war?"

"I don't understand it either, but I have faith that God knows what He is doing."

Benjamin Spock, the noted pediatrician, suggests that parents answer questions about God and the Bible and heaven along the following lines: "The Bible is a book that was written thousands of years ago. It tells how God made the whole world in the beginning. It says He made the sun and the moon and the stars, and the mountains and the oceans. It says He made all the animals and birds and fishes, and finally people. Lots of people go to synagogue or church to sing songs to God, to thank Him for all

the good things they have, like delicious food and a nice house
and warm clothes. They also ask God to help them be good. The
Bible says God lives in heaven, but we don't know where that
is. Some say it's in the sky. People can't really see God. But they
feel He's there just the same, not as a body, but as a spirit.''

THE MEANING
OF DEATH

*I would tell my children there's a baby on the way. We would
talk about names for boys or girls; we would talk about
whether we should paint the bedroom pink or blue—or if
you're not sure, yellow. It's the most normal thing in the
world.*

*If we can talk about death the same way, then I think we
would live differently.*

—ELISABETH KÜBLER-ROSS, M.D.

Most of us ignore, deny, or otherwise avoid the thought of death.
To think about death means to admit that life will end for each
of us. Many people find this concept anxiety-provoking. But death
is a fact of life that we must all come to terms with. As an ancient
Turkish proverb puts it: "Death is a black camel that kneels once
at every man's door." Fortunately, our society is beginning to
recognize that treating death as a taboo does a disservice to both
the dying and the living, adding to loneliness, anxiety, and stress
for all of us. Efforts are now under way to remove the topic of
death from the same closet that previously housed the unspeak-
able subject of sex.

Contrary to popular belief, most children and adolescents
want to talk about death with their parents. Children are very
much concerned with death. The question of life and death is
part of their continuous search for meaning. "Why do people
and animals die?" is a common question. When surveyed, most
children report that death is rarely, if ever, discussed in their
family. Most parents admit "severe problems" in discussing
questions related to death and dying. However, when parents
ignore children's questions, or mislead them, they only confuse
the children or make them anxious. The way to make death less

mysterious and frightening to children is to openly discuss the topic with them.

A CHILD'S CONCEPT OF DEATH

Research indicates that children go through a series of stages in their understanding of death. As they develop, their understanding of death becomes more differentiated and realistic. In talking to your child about death, you should proceed slowly, step by step, according to the child's level of understanding.

Below age two, there is no understanding of death. At each level of development after this, children will take in what information they can about death, and gradually their understanding will increase.

Ages three to five.   A preschooler knows death is somehow connected with sadness. Most preschoolers regard life and death as related to mobility: moving means life; lack of movement means death. Death is not perceived as a final event, but as a temporary and reversible happening. Watching cartoon characters rise up again after being completely crushed tends to reinforce this notion. Preschoolers tend to wonder what the deceased is eating or whether a dead person is afraid to be in the dark underground. The fear of death at this age centers on separation from needed parents. Anger at a deceased parent for leaving is to be expected.

Ages six to eight.   The six-to-eight-year-olds are beginning to realize the finality of death. They tend to personify death, which means they associate it with a skeleton, a monster, or a ghostlike figure such as the grim reaper. This often leads to nightmares and fear of the dark. The child this age often does not comprehend the inevitability of his own death. When a loved one dies, the child may feel it is a punishment for his own bad thoughts or deeds.

Ages nine through twelve. From nine or ten through adolescence, children begin to realize fully that death is irreversible, universal, and inevitable, that all living things die, and that they, too, will die someday.

They understand this as an inevitable process that happens to people according to certain physical laws: e.g., sometimes the body wears out just like an old car and can't run any longer ("like the withering of flowers") or at other times the body reacts to injuries inflicted upon it.

HOW TO TELL CHILDREN ABOUT DEATH

What you say to your children about death will depend on many things, including your own beliefs about death, and the children's level of understanding. There are, however, some guidelines that people have found useful in giving sound, meaningful answers to children's questions about death. Your goal in talking about death is for children to view it as a natural and nonfrightening event, and to be prepared for inevitable death experiences, such as the loss of a grandparent.

Be concrete. Since children under the age of nine have difficulty understanding abstract concepts, be simple and direct. Relate your answers to a child's own experiences. So explain death to young children in terms of the *absence of familiar life functions*—a dead person does not breathe, talk, feel, sleep, or need food; a dog does not bark or run anymore. If your five-year-old asks, "What is dead, Mommy?" you might respond, "Dead means not to be alive anymore. It's like those flowers that faded; their life was ended. The body doesn't work anymore when it's dead. It doesn't move, or hear, or breathe, or feel, or even sleep. It just stops."

You might also point out that you will not see a dead person or pet again. If the child asks where the person will live, you might say "in our hearts" or "in our minds"; if you're a religious person, you could say "in heaven" or "with God."

The following conversation illustrates how one mother helped her four-year-old daughter understand the death of her dog:

"Mommy, Tora won't get up."

"Tora is dead, Karine. He died. He won't ever get up again."

"Dead?"

"Yes, that's right. Dead."

"What's dead?"

"Dead means that Tora has stopped breathing, and his heart has stopped beating. See how he's not moving? He'll never be able to move again."

"How come?"

"Because sooner or later everything that lives has to die."

"Now make Tora better."

"I'm sorry, honey, I can't make Tora better. This isn't like when your scooter broke and I fixed it. Or like when you had a stomachache and Daddy gave you medicine to make you feel better. This is different. When you're dead you can't be fixed."

"Why?"

"Because that's the way things are. Remember how we planted seeds in the garden last spring?"

"Yes."

"And remember how they grew and became beautiful flowers?"

"Yes."

"And then after a while all the flowers fell off and never came back. Remember?"

"Yes."

"Well, that's what this is like. Tora used to be a little puppy.

Then he grew up to be a big dog and had lots of fun with us for a while. Then he got old, and now he's dead."

Be comfortable thinking and talking about death. Each of us must accept and make our peace with death. As soon as a parent can accept death, intellectually and emotionally, the child will start to feel more comfortable with it. Death should not be considered a frightening or morbid topic of conversation. We should be as willing to talk to our children about death as about birth.

Introduce children to the idea of death at an early age. A child's learning about the meaning of death should be gradual and part of everyday experiences. The simplest way to introduce children to the concept of death is to talk openly about the natural life cycle of flowers, insects, and animals. Give your children the opportunities to be responsible for the care of pets, plants, and insects. Encourage children to observe the natural stages of the birth, growth, reproduction, and death of these living things. Explain that all living things age continuously from birth, and eventually die. In this way they make room for new living things to take their place on earth. So the fact that living things—including people—die will be as natural as the fact that they are born. Accept a child's questions as they come, with an attitude of "I won't know all the answers, but it's O.K. to ask."

Be accurate in your explanations. By being presented factually and straightforwardly, death becomes less mysterious and frightening to a child. Use proper words such as "death" and "dead" and not euphemistic terms which may confuse a child, such as "passed away" or "expired." Take all questions about death and dying seriously and respond honestly to each.

Avoid denial, subterfuge, and "myths" (beliefs in an afterlife you
do not hold).

   Listen to your child.   Take time to understand what your
child is asking about death. Answer a young child's specific questions without adding further information which is not requested.
This avoids overwhelming a child. For example, you might respond to the question "Will I die when I grow up?" by simply
stating that everyone dies someday. In response to "Are you
going to die too?" reassure the child by saying you expect to go
on living with the child for a long time. When asked why a
specific person in mourning is crying, you might say something
like: "Aunt Ethel is crying because she is sad that Uncle Joe has
died. She misses him very much. We all feel sad when someone
we care about dies."

   Teach gradually.   Don't try to explain death in one discussion. Remember that children learn through repetition, so
they may have to hear the same question answered over and
over again. As they grow older and more mature, children will
need further clarification and elaboration.

   Ask for feedback.   With young children, it's a good idea
to ask the child to explain back again what he has been told.
This offers the opportunity to correct any gross distortions or
misperceptions.

HOW NOT TO TELL CHILDREN ABOUT DEATH

The following are some ineffective ways to discuss death:
   Don't equate death with sleep, lest your child start to fear
sleep. So don't use metaphors such as someone went "to sleep"
or to their "eternal rest." If your children confuse death with

sleep, they may become afraid of going to bed or taking naps, since they may fear they won't wake up.

Don't say someone who died "went away" or on a "long, long trip." The child may feel deserted or wonder why the person did not say goodbye. Also, the child may fear that other adults who go away, for a vacation or another reason, may not return either.

Don't tell young children that someone died because he got "sick." Preschoolers cannot tell the difference between temporary and terminal illness, and minor ailments may start to worry them. With young children, it is best to explain that only a very serious sickness can cause death, and that although we all get a little sick at times, we quickly recover from these minor ailments.

Don't say, "Only old people die," since your child is likely to discover that young people die too. It is better to say something like: "Most people live a long time, but some don't. I expect you and I will."

Don't say, "God took Grandpa away because he loved him so." Such a comment implies that all of us left living are not loved as much.

Don't say, "God took your sister because she was so good." If being good means you have to leave the family forever, then the child may decide to be bad.

Don't forbid a child to grieve, by saying, "Be brave, show us how strong you can be." Let a child cry for the loss of a loved one.

Don't avoid the issue, that is, be unwilling to acknowledge or do anything about a child's death experiences and questions.

Don't tell a child how to feel: e.g., "You shouldn't be upset— it's God's will."

Don't postpone helping a child handle death experiences by waiting until the child brings the subject up.

Don't rush to the pet store to replace a dead hamster. This denies your child the opportunity to understand and accept death. Let your child see and touch a dead pet. She needs to learn to face the reality of death and to mourn. This will prepare her to cope with the subsequent deaths of relatives and friends.

WAR AND NUCLEAR WEAPONS

Warfare is as old as human history. Since it is still prevalent among nations, children's understanding of it begins to develop early. By age six, children are talking about war and peace, and by age seven or eight, they have fairly well defined ideas about their meaning. At this age, children can understand that nations go to war primarily to defend themselves—they feel their national existence, honor, power, or influence is threatened in some way. Preadolescence (ages eleven to thirteen) is a particularly important time for the development of attitudes about war. Children this age tend to have fewer ideas about peace as an active process than they do about war.

It is a natural biological tendency of man to respond in an aggressive way to threat. However, we must make it clear to our children that war is not a necessary mode of conflict resolution. Nations can learn to settle their differences in nonviolent ways by mutual understanding, negotiation, and arbitration. The inhumanity and horror of war must be made clear to children of all nations.

We must stop teaching our children that our enemies are invariably treacherous, cruel, and warlike, while we are invariably peace-loving, honorable, and humane. Such black-and-white thinking will only convince children that war is inevitable and necessary. People of all nations are both loving and aggressive. We must look for the good in others and find ways to work together in peace and cooperation.

NUCLEAR WAR

Since we live in a nuclear age, the threat of nuclear holocaust is an ever-present concern. Yet few parents or teachers talk to children about the possibility of a nuclear disaster. Until recently, to talk about the bomb was so threatening in our society that it was generally regarded as an antisocial act.

A study entitled "The Impact of Nuclear Developments on Children and Adolescents" was recently conducted by two Harvard University psychiatrists. This and other studies reveal that parents and children generally try not to think about the possibility of nuclear war because it is so catastrophic. A kind of "psychic numbing" results, in which there is a diminished capacity to feel that allows us not to experience the fearful reality. The emotions become anesthetized so the psyche does not become overwhelmed with emotional distress. But denial does not work for many children and "nuclear anxiety" is manifested in a variety of ways, such as nightmares, and somatic complaints. Some teenagers state that they don't want to bring up children in a world at the brink of madness and holocaust.

HOPE VERSUS DESPAIR

"Family nuclear syndrome" is a term used by psychiatrists to describe the situation in which there is a pervasive despair in the family about the futility of planning for the future. There is a general feeling of gloom because the bomb might fall any day. Symptoms include deep and unspecified fears, chronic anxiety, impotent rage, and, most of all, a fatalistic "live for today" attitude. Not seeing a secure future, some young people turn to hedonistic behaviors such as drug use and sexual promiscuity; others turn to more direct self-destructive behaviors, such as suicide. The family nuclear syndrome thrives in homes where the parents repeatedly talk of war, pestilence, and nuclear issues in a depressed, fatalistic way.

To prevent the family nuclear syndrome from occurring, parents need to give their children visions of promise in the future. So avoid being overly gloomy—i.e., a doomsayer. The following myth underscores the importance of hope in our lives:

According to the Pandora myth, the god Jupiter was angry

at Prometheus for stealing fire from the gods to benefit mankind. To get even, he sent Pandora to earth carrying a box which she was warned not to open. Overcome by curiosity, she lifted its cover just a little and instantly a swarm of plagues flew out. Pandora slammed the lid shut as fast as she could, but only one thing was left in the box—and that was hope. Hope, according to the myth, is what makes the rest of our human cares and troubles bearable.

Hope and despair activate the dynamics of self-fulfilling prophecies. Hopeful people may realize their hopes because hope gives impetus to their active strivings; the despairing are all too likely to be confirmed in their fears by the passivity that fatalism justifies.

Since hope/despair is the sentiment that connects present and future for people, it is central to people's morale. So parents should remain hopeful about the future of the world and convey this hope to their children. If you react with courage and hope to the nuclear threat, your children will most likely follow your example.

OPEN COMMUNICATION

Apart from instilling hope, parents need to talk with their children to help them cope with the threat of nuclear war. Experts agree that the best way is not to try to shield them from awareness, but to give knowledge and understanding. It is not helpful to tell your children not to worry, that a horrible disaster will not happen. The battle to blot out the bitter truth is inevitably a losing one. It is only a matter of time until some terrifying image, some deadly bit of information, will leap out from the television or the news headlines. We must deal with the nuclear issue openly and honestly and break down the conspiracy of silence which has existed for too long. Younger and younger children are becoming concerned with these issues, since they see it on the media.

How you should talk about war and nuclear weapons will depend on the age of the child.

Preschoolers basically just want to know that you are aware of the threat and will take care of them. Your answers should be brief and supportive. Be optimistic that nations will learn to settle their disputes peacefully.

School-age children want more information than younger children. Don't suppress talk about their nuclear fears or avoid discussions. Instead, say, "Yes, I know you're afraid, and I've been thinking about this too. I know it's scary, but here's what I think and what can be done so it won't happen."

An open discussion of the issues can clear up misunderstandings and can make things less frightening. Put the threat in context. Most nations won't use the bomb since retaliation is so certain. Also, point out to them that though we live in a dangerous world, nuclear war is not inevitable, necessary, or even very likely. Mankind has rid itself of other pandemics, like smallpox, the plague, slavery, and burning witches. We can also rid ourselves of the current irrationality that underlies the proliferation of nuclear weapons. Millions of people throughout the world are working actively to prevent a nuclear catastrophe from engulfing humanity. Discuss some of the specific organizations that have been formed and their concrete recommendations for solutions, such as a bilateral nuclear weapons freeze, followed by a reduction in nuclear armaments.

Suggest to your older children that they might want to start thinking of solutions and to actively try to do something about it. Some children have started a letter-writing exchange with peers in the Soviet Union, in the hope of forming friendship and promoting understanding.

You can be a role model for your children by taking action yourself. You can initiate some political action to halt the armaments race by participating in demonstrations, writing letters to your representatives in Congress, or joining a study group.

FINAL THOUGHTS

As parents, we have the responsibility to help children understand
the unacceptability of nuclear war. That trust and cooperation
is possible among the peoples of the world is evidenced by the
undeniable progress of civilization since the beginning of man,
by many recent activities of the United Nations and the World
Health Organization, and the increasing participation of millions
of persons in movements toward peace and friendship.

MONEY AND WORK

In many ways, money is as sensitive a topic in the home as sex. Most parents seem to believe that their children will learn the value of money by osmosis. Yet the pressures and complexities of our moneyed world have never been greater. Parents need to give their children sound attitudes and values toward money, along with experience in managing it sensibly.

ATTITUDES AND VALUES

Before we can give our children a healthy attitude toward money, we need to examine what meaning money has for us. We live in a society which is used to spending and possessing material things. Unless good sense is used in placing the proper value on money, one can become obsessed with keeping up with the Joneses. Money has long been a symbol of power, security, and prestige. Many people see it as a primary measure of self-worth. So it is easy to overvalue money and see it as the key to everything desirable. The common expression "Money isn't everything" reflects the recognition that some things in life cannot be bought. One needs to keep the right balance between material things and other values, such as love, friendship, appreciation of beauty, and religion. Once parents have money and the things it can buy in proper perspective, they will be able to help their children with this topic.

Try to make money a discussible topic in your home. Many children have a limited notion of money and retain the impression that their parents can buy everything they want. You don't need to tell them exactly how much you earn, but let them know where you stand financially and show them where the money goes. Talk to your children about how much money you spend every month on food, rent, and utilities. Discuss the risks and

131

advantages of credit cards and savings programs. Include them in family financial decisions such as whether to redecorate the living room or use the money to go on a family vacation. Encourage your children to voice their opinions on such matters.

Besides verbal discussions, you convey the meaning of money in other ways. It is important to avoid the habit of giving material things to your children as the way you express love and affection. If money becomes a substitute for a loving relationship, children are apt to overvalue money (hoard it) or disdain it (become big spenders). Such children may also try to buy the friendship of their peers with money—much as their parents have done with them. Parents should also keep praise and criticism separate from money so children don't equate it with acceptance. Don't take away a child's allowance as a punishment.

MONEY MANAGEMENT

Children need to understand how to manage money just as they must learn other skills for living. Studies have shown that children who know the most about money are those who are given wide experience in spending it and opportunities to save it.

Saving.   Children five and under seek immediate gratification of their impulses, so don't expect them to have the desire to save their money or to appreciate its importance. Once they enter elementary school, however, children should be encouraged to save their money for an item they desire, such as a baseball glove or a trip to an amusement park. But don't *insist* that the child save his allowance or gifts. This really means you are saving for him. Since the child has no choice in the matter, he is not learning a lesson.

Allowance.   Starting about age five or six, children should have an allowance. By giving them a regular allowance you teach them to make their own decisions and to realize that when they've spent their money, there isn't any more. It is only by making choices and living with the consequences that children learn to develop sound judgment. When you go shopping, encourage your children to bring some of their own money in case they want to buy something. When it's their own money they are spending, they are more likely to think twice about what they're spending it on.

The amount of the allowance will depend on how old and responsible the child is, and what expenses you expect the allowance to cover. Sit down with your child and make a list of all the expenses she will be responsible for. Help the child keep a list of actual expenses for a few weeks. This record-keeping will assist in determining how large the allowance should be. The allowance should include both earmarked money and money to spend as the child wishes. As the child grows older, parents should increase the number of items the allowance must cover. Be calm about mistakes the child makes in spending the allowance. A ten-dollar error now is better than a thousand-dollar mistake later.

Linking allowances to chores or grades is not wise. Children should be expected to do household chores because, as members of a family, they have certain everyday responsibilities—not because they're going to get paid. Parents should, however, give their children a chance to earn extra money for doing chores beyond their usual household duties.

WORK

Work attitudes, values, and habits are developed to a significant degree during the elementary-school years. Home chores and schoolwork are as much work as is work in paid employment. Parents must make a conscious, systematic effort to set a positive example of good work attitudes and habits. Be organized and thorough in your work at home. Strive for excellence in your performance. Express enthusiasm, pride, and satisfaction in your work, even at the most menial of tasks. By being dependable and working hard at home, you will help your children develop a work ethic.

The guiding principle we all should follow in approaching work was aptly stated by Henry Giles:

"Man must work. That is certain as the sun. But he may work grudgingly or he may work gratefully; he may work as a man, or he may work as a machine. There is no work so rude, that he may not exalt it; no work so impassive, that he may not breathe a soul into it; no work so dull, that he may not enliven it."

CHORES

Some work seems to be a natural part of one's responsibility in the family, such as making one's bed and cleaning one's room. Other work, such as mowing the lawn, cleaning, or painting, may fit in the compensation category. Parents need to determine for their own family which work fits into which category.

Some guidelines on making household chores a positive work experience for children are:

- Give your child a choice of several jobs. Let the personality and likes of the child influence the choice.
- Don't palm off all the unpleasant work on the children. If you don't like to clean the bathroom, chances are the children will dislike it also. Mutual compromise is needed here. Perhaps rotating the tasks is the best solution.
- Complete some chores together. This will give you a chance to relate to the child and model effective work habits and attitudes.
- Express praise and appreciation for your child's work efforts at home.
- If your child fails to do a required chore, withhold a privilege such as TV watching or fun activities until the work is done.

PREJUDICE

Most Americans agree that prejudice is bad and that children should be taught to avoid it. Prejudice refers to a judgment or opinion formed before the facts are known, literally a prejudgment that is not based on knowledge.

Prejudice leads to intolerance and hatred of other races, creeds, and religions. It is directly counter to the American democratic creed, which is to treat every person according to his or her individual characteristics, rather than according to race, sex, social class, religion, or national origin. America was founded on a belief in the equality and brotherhood of man.

Without a doubt, prejudices flourish today, handed down from generation to generation. Children are not born with prejudice. They learn it gradually while growing up, from the society they live in. Children begin their learning at an early age; by kindergarten, most children show a clear preference for children of their own race. Although there are many reasons for prejudice, one of the most satisfying advantages derived from it is the boost to one's self-esteem derived from feeling superior to other people. During economic hard times, when many people suffer from bruised egos, bigotry tends to thrive.

There are four main ways to head off bigotry in children: set a good example, supply information, encourage contact, and speak out.

SET AN EXAMPLE

The first thing to do is to become fully aware of our own prejudices, since all of us have some. So tune in to the prejudicial attitudes that you hold and ask yourself if they are what you want to convey. If not, make a conscious effort to think and act in a different, more humane way. Control any inclinations you have to make disparaging remarks about people different from you. Try to act differently as well. Cultivate friends and acquaintances from other racial, religious, and ethnic groups. Be active in democratic undertakings which work against discriminatory practices in the community.

PROVIDE INFORMATION

Next, it is wise to talk to your children from an early age about prejudice. By taking a clear stance against prejudice, you may be able to prevent prejudicial ideas from taking root in the minds of your preschoolers. A child old enough to ask questions about problems of race, religion, or nationality is old enough to receive honest and appropriate answers.

Some kinds of information that you could provide to combat prejudice are:

- Point out that the ways people are similar are really more fundamental than the ways they differ. The human capacities for thought, love, and feelings are really more important for judging the worth of a man than such superficial characteristics as skin color.
- In the American tradition of pluralism, help your children to value diversity by regarding differences in culture, physical appearance, and religions as attractive distinctions that add interest and a welcome variety to human interactions. Tell about the historical, cultural, and economic factors that determine why various groups are the way they are and behave the way they do.
- Discuss how unreasonable it is to discriminate or treat others unfairly because of unimportant differences such as skin color or physical handicaps. Mention the lack of proof of inborn superiority of any one group over any other, and the wide individual differences within every racial, religious, and national group. Talk with your children about the achievements of outstanding individuals in all groups.

- The misinformation in stereotypes should be challenged, such as the beliefs that "the Irish are drunks" or "the Jews are money grubbers." Point out the flaws in these gross overgeneralizations.
- Mention the advances made in the last few decades to reduce prejudice, such as the decline in overt racism against blacks.

ENCOURAGE COOPERATIVE CONTACT

Studies have shown that when children live, work, or play together in equality, they learn how similar they really are in their personal beliefs, their likes and dislikes. They tend to discover their common humanity. So encourage firsthand contact with members of different groups through such means as school activities or sports. Contact is most effective in reducing prejudice when it occurs under conditions of equal status, such as members of a team working together toward a common goal.

SPEAK OUT

Take a strong and determined stance against disparaging remarks made by others (including your family) in fun or seriousness against any race, religion, or other "different" group. Be open and firm in exposing prejudices.

In addition, encourage your children to stand up at an early age, verbally and openly, against the prejudicial behavior of others. Teach them to do it in the least offensive way, but to do it.

PREJUDICE TOWARD THE HANDICAPPED

A handicapped person is someone who has a persistent physical or mental defect which interferes with his functioning successfully and with satisfaction in daily living.

Children with physical, mental, or emotional handicaps are often the victims of prejudice and discrimination in many areas.

The number of handicapped children in our society is about one in ten. Even though these special-needs children have handicaps which interfere with everyday life and performance, they are more like other children than they are different. They are first of all persons, with all the feelings, interests, and attitudes of others. The handicapping condition is just one aspect of the child's total picture of strengths and weaknesses.

So teach your children to be understanding and appreciative of the handicapped rather than pitying or disparaging. In addition, we all must work toward removing barriers to educational, occupational, and housing opportunities for the handicapped. They must be allowed to enter society in every respect, limited only by whatever specific handicap may be involved. Above all, we must treat them as persons equal in worth, rights, and dignity to us.

PREJUDICE TOWARD WOMEN

The prejudice against females is still very strong in our society. Many girls wonder if they are valued by their parents as much as their brothers are. What can parents do about this? First of all, love and value your children equally and let them know you do. Explain that boys and girls can do many of the same things equally well. Don't assign chores by gender. Don't channel a girl's career aspirations to stereotypes such as nurses, secretaries, housewives, and airplane stewardesses. Point out that women do equally well as physicians, Supreme Court justices, politicians, bankers, engineers, pilots, and sportscasters.

Ask your children how they think boys and girls compare to one another in intelligence, personality, and interests. If they have prejudicial notions, set them straight—not critically but in an instructive way.

PREJUDICE TOWARD OLD PEOPLE

Ask children what thoughts come to mind when you say the word "old," and the chances are that their associations will all be negative, such as "crippled," "death," "bent," and "rusty."

In America, the idea has long been fostered that "being old" is synonymous with "being through." A stigma has become attached to the aging process. On the balance sheet, nothing is added for knowledge and wisdom gained through years of experience.

One of our greatest natural resources is our older, more experienced population. We can learn a lot from them, and none of us are so wise that we don't need their counsel. We have got to show children by our actions that old people have a valuable contribution to make and that their efforts are valued.

As parents, we need to actively assist our children in discovering and appreciating the value of older persons. How can we do this? First, we must give them some positive thoughts to balance the negative images of aging which abound and make it difficult for children to see the value in society's elders. One way is to relate your own memories of your grandparents as understanding, helpful, wise, and loving.

In addition, parents must endeavor to bring the young and the old together in joint activities. By encouraging this bond between young and old, parents will help build respect in children for age and thus undermine society's prejudice.

The very young and the very old go together naturally. Old people are so important to the young that children who don't have grandparents sometimes "adopt" an older companion. Old people can play special roles for the young, among them: living ancestor and historian—responsible for passing along family history; nurturer—someone present early in a child's life and available in later years to offer support if needed; and role model—to help guide young people.

RISK-TAKING
AND FAILURE

A man's success is made up of failures, because he experiments and ventures every day, and the more falls he gets, moves faster on. . . . I have heard that in horsemanship he is not the good rider who never was thrown, but rather that a man will never be a good rider until he is thrown; then he will not be haunted any longer by the terror that he shall tumble, and will ride whither he is bound.
—RALPH WALDO EMERSON

The tragedy of our times is that our young people are being taught that they must never make a mistake—that to make a mistake is unforgivable. All great men have made mistakes. If you're afraid of making a mistake, then it means you will stop functioning.
—ELEANOR ROOSEVELT

Occasional failure is the price of progress. If you never try anything new—if you never consider anything that might possibly fail—how can you possibly improve your methods and results? Clearly, it is better to try and fail than to not risk trying at all. People who stand still may avoid stubbing their toes, but they won't make much progress. High achievers are those with the courage to try new ideas and run the risk of making mistakes.

Exceptional individuals like Picasso, Einstein, and Mother Teresa were able to sustain themselves in their developing years with few successes, amid, probably, a multitude of failures. Anyone who sets his goals high is bound to have a certain number of failures. Babe Ruth set a record for home runs. He also set a record for strikeouts. But he didn't let that worry him—he just kept on swinging for the fences!

So high achievement is the result of continuous effort and

repeated failure. The line between failure and success is so fine that we scarcely realize when we pass it; so fine that we are often on the line and do not know it. Many people throw up their hands at a time when a little more effort, a little more patience, would achieve success. Others avoid trying in the first place because of fear of failure. They view failures and mistakes as "catastrophes" rather than as steps on the path to eventual success. Children who learn to set their goals high and persevere at a task despite repeated failures are well on their way to making maximum use of their talents.

TEACHING CHILDREN HOW TO FAIL

Most children fear failure because they have not learned to make failure a growth experience. So teaching children how to fail successfully is an important responsibility of parenthood.

Failure is never pleasurable. It is painful for children and adults alike. After he lost the presidential election in 1952, Adlai Stevenson said he was "too old to cry, but it hurt too much to laugh." But failure can be a positive experience if one does the following:

First ask, "Why did I fail?" Overcome the impulse to blame someone else. Ask what *you* did wrong, and how *you* can improve. So try to learn something from the failure that will sharpen your judgment the next time around.

Second, it is important to realize that failing at one or two things does not make one a failure. Perfectionists feel their self-worth depends on external factors such as being successful at everything they do. So they do not face up to their shortcomings or failures.

Children need to learn and accept the fact that no one can be best at everything, no one can win all the time—and that it is possible to enjoy a game even when you don't win. In short, it is human to fail and make mistakes, and this imperfection does not diminish our self-worth.

RISK-TAKING

To take a risk is to expose oneself to failure or danger or rejection. On the other hand, it can lead to excitement, acceptance, and success. We grow through risking, through trying new things, and parents are in a key position to encourage sensible risking.

There are three approaches to taking risks: overly cautious, reckless, and reasonable.

Overly cautious.   The overly cautious person seeks security and the status quo. Rather than take chances, this person prefers to stay in the "comfort zone"—a safe, secure environment—even when it means mediocrity and boredom. Parents who are too perfectionist and set standards that are too high tend to produce children who are afraid to fail.

This outlook can also be fostered by parents who communicate to a child that the world is full of dangers and that to fail or make a mistake is awful. Consequently, the child diligently seeks security, comfort, and protection.

Reckless.   The reckless person is noted for fearless, daredevil behaviors. This person takes unreasonable risks which involve putting oneself in a situation where nothing positive can be gained, where one can lose something of value which can't be replaced, or where serious physical or mental harm can result to oneself or to another person.

Some examples of unreasonable risks are:

- Taking so much of anything that you develop a psychological dependence on it (cigarettes, alcohol, food).
- Not going to the doctor when you are really sick.
- Stealing.
- Driving a car while drunk, or riding with a drunk driver
- Darting in and out of traffic on roller skates.

- Skiing on an advanced slope when you are only a beginner.
- Betting money that you can't afford to lose.
- Playing Russian roulette with a loaded revolver.

Reasonable. A reasonable risk exists when the possible benefits outweigh the potential loss. People who are good risk-takers have the courage to bet on their abilities and ideas, to take calculated risks and to act.

If your child is considering a decision involving an element of risk, ask the child:

- What are the chances of succeeding in this choice?
- Do you understand the risk?
- Are you willing to take a risk? Consider the worst and ask yourself how you would cope with it. Could you live with it? If not, don't take the chance.
- Would it be better to find another alternative, with a lower risk factor?
- Does the potential benefit justify the risk?

The following case illustrates a reasonable risk. Charles Lindbergh's boys once asked his permission to climb an awesomely tall tree. He responded, "How are you going up?" Scott, the twelve-year-old, pointed: first this limb, then that. "You're going to get stuck after that, aren't you?" Lindbergh prodded. The boys sadly agreed. Only when they had calculated their chances on various routes up the tree did their father give his consent. Then, to a watching friend, he said, "They must learn to take calculated risks. As long as they figure out everything ahead of time and just don't go off half-cocked."

Some families adopt an overprotective approach which is likely to make children feel weak and vulnerable. Charlie Shedd, the newspaper columnist, once told about parents who refused to allow their son to try out for catcher on the school baseball team. They immediately said, "No. What if you get hurt?" One night at the dinner table, the son expressed his pent-up feelings: "You make me so mad. You won't let me do anything. I couldn't go skiing because I might break a leg. Couldn't take jumping lessons at the stable; the horse might fall. And last summer I couldn't even go canoeing on vacation with those kids from Minnesota. What if we tipped over? You've always been like that with everything that's fun. I don't think you're one bit fair. And what I really think is I might as well be dead too." His parents thought over these remarks and admitted their mistake. They had lost their first child shortly after birth and were thus over-protecting their only remaining child. Given the opportunity, he soon excelled at baseball.

SPORTS

Physical and sports activities are part of a child's everyday experience. Early and enjoyable sports experiences can help children develop positive attitudes toward fitness and health, provide lasting patterns of recreational activity, and foster development of such highly regarded behaviors as achievement motivation, assertiveness, persistence, cooperativeness, and the ability to cope with pressure and competition anxiety. Even more important to young children, they can provide a great deal of fun.

How can parents guide their children to use sports to add to their pleasure in life and their physical well-being? The following are some guidelines.

ENCOURAGEMENT VERSUS PRESSURE

A basic principle is to encourage your child to pursue athletic interests and develop innate talents, but to avoid pressuring the child. Encouragement involves providing children with the knowledge, training, and equipment they need to develop basic physical skills. Early success can be a positive reinforcement for children and keep them at an athletic task voluntarily. Parental interest and praise are also important aspects of encouragement.

Undue pressure, on the other hand, can result from a failure of parents to differentiate their own goals from those of their children. Too many parents become overly involved in a child's talent because they derive self-esteem and excitement from it. So be sure your child has the motivation to do well in a sport, as opposed to just your desiring it.

Don't push your children into sports they don't enjoy, or to levels of performance that are beyond them. If a child feels compelled to participate in a sport, her chances of enjoying it and being successful at it are diminished. Also, help your child develop realistic expectations about her athletic abilities. A child who aims too high is often disappointed, for even when playing well, she will remain dissatisfied. A child who matures early may be initially better at sports. However, others will soon catch up. This could be a serious blow to the early maturer's self-esteem.

COMPETITIVE SPORTS

Competition can be healthy if it pushes one to one's maximum capacity for excellence and superior performance. However, it becomes destructive when the main focus is to triumph over someone else or to avoid losing at all costs.

In sports, the emphasis on winning has increased in the last decade because the rewards are so much greater, particularly the financial ones for top athletes. Because of this, there seem to be fewer displays of sportsmanship and fair play. Examples of unsportsmanlike conduct are abundant in the media, including cheating (spitballs by pitchers), unnecessary roughness, and verbal abuse of umpires and linesmen. Parents and coaches need to openly express their disapproval of these and other unsportsmanlike behaviors, such as taunting losing teams, breaking rules of the game, indulging in temper outbursts, and blaming others for one's shortcomings or defeats.

Remember that your child is not *born* with unhealthy competitive qualities; it's *learned* behavior. And much of it comes from watching *your* reactions to competition, both actively and passively as a spectator. Instead of asking your child, "Did you win?" when he comes in the door, ask him, "Did you have fun?" or "Did you play well?"

Some early-warning signs of overcompetitiveness in child sports are:

- Unusually intense and prolonged anger or depression after a loss. If negative feelings last an entire day, it's being taken too seriously.

- Tantrums on the court or playing field, attempts at cheating, or putting down losing teams.
- Extreme nervousness, hours or days before a competition. Anxiety attacks do not enhance the quality of life for a child.

AGGRESSIVENESS

Aggressive sports—that is, ones that are likely to result in physical injury to oneself or others—have been found to heighten violence among viewers and participants. So don't encourage a child who tends to be aggressive to engage in sports that place a premium on aggression, such as hockey and football. Quite possibly these sports will reward a child for being aggressive and may lead him to carry over the behavior to areas where it is inappropriate. Try to direct an aggressive child to less violent sports, such as golf and tennis.

TIME COMMITMENT

How much time should a child spend on sports? First of all, single-minded devotion to an activity can produce children who are addicted and obsessed with sports and winning. The time spent on sports must be weighed against that for other important activities, such as friendship and schooling. In making a decision, one should also consider how much inconvenience it will mean for family mealtimes, vacation times, and weekends. A family should not be made to revolve around a child's talent, nor should it be pauperized because of it. A sane balance of priorities must be made between sports involvement and a fulfilling life outside of sports for the child and the family. Of course, to develop a child's talent to a professional level, a great deal of dedication, practice, and professional instruction must be present. Some sacrifices will have to be made by the child and the family.

MUSIC LESSONS

Music can play an important part in the lives of children. It can contribute to their physical, emotional, intellectual, and aesthetic development. The task of a parent is to guide a child to discover her own musical interests and talents, and to make her own decisions about pursuing musical activities. Most children have some degree of responsiveness to music and this can be encouraged and developed. A child does not have to possess a special "talent" to profit from musical experiences and lessons. Early exposure to music can stimulate increased musical understanding and heightened appreciation in a child. These experiences should include a variety of both listening and participation activities. Play your favorite records and instruments, visit music shops, and attend musical productions.

Parents often have many questions and concerns about music lessons for their children. The main concern is whether one should insist on lessons for a reluctant child. It seems best not to force lessons on a child. Instead, expose your child to the different types of instruments and offer to provide lessons. Typically, children quit music lessons within three to six months. They get discouraged because practicing is tedious and the successes do not come as fast as imagined. So when your child first takes lessons, don't worry about immediate results. Rather, motivate your child to "stick with it" for at least a year. Then let the child quit if she wants to. But if your child is really talented, encourage her not to make the decision overnight.

When should music lessons begin? Generally, children start lessons at about age seven or eight, when they have mastered basic reading. But a child's interest in music, attention span, and eagerness to learn are the best indications of readiness.

Remember that most children like to first learn a musical instrument through group play in a school band or orchestra. The feeling of being part of a group motivates them to endure the tediousness of beginning lessons. Encourage practice at home by posting a schedule and have your child record daily practice time. Attend recitals in which your child participates whenever you're invited. Your presence is a demonstration of interest and support.

Every child will have to decide for himself if he wants to succeed at music. To be successful at music will require concentrated effort. This is one of the reasons that children who do well in music often achieve academic success as well. The habits of self-discipline that they learn in music carry over into other areas of their lives. They acquire the confidence to master difficult tasks and to pursue challenging goals.

SANTA CLAUS

Studies indicate that about 90 percent of Christian mothers clearly believe the Santa Claus myth is desirable and encourage their young children to believe in it. Some parents, however, have mixed emotions about telling their children about Santa Claus and other mythical figures of childhood. They wonder if it is wrong to lie to children and if basic trust will be lost when children learn the truth. Will Santa make it more difficult for children to distinguish fact from fantasy?

Most experts on child development consider such doubts needless. The inevitable realization of the mythical nature of these beliefs will not destroy trust in parents, since many other incidents prove the credibility of one's parents.

Some child development specialists contend that refusing to let a child believe in Santa Claus may be harmful, since the child may feel strange and alienated as the only skeptic in his class. Fantasy and make-believe are natural to childhood and they foster a healthy development of children's imaginative thinking. There is no need to get too realistic with young children, who enjoy fantasies and fairy tales of different types.

What does a belief in Santa, the Easter Bunny, and the Tooth Fairy add to childhood? First, such beliefs add excitement, wonder, and enjoyment to life. They also make children feel less obligated to their parents for all things. Children like to think there are others in the world who will do things for them.

According to Bruno Bettelheim, author of *The Uses of Enchantment,* the Santa Claus myth is not harmful to children and is a very enjoyable experience for them. To force them to give up this fantasy too early, he believes, is a needless deprivation.

WHEN TO ADMIT THERE IS NO SANTA

Research indicates that most children give up the belief in Santa between the ages of four and eight. One study of middle-class children from Christian families revealed that at age four, about 85 percent of children believe in Santa. At age eight, only 25 percent still really believe, 55 percent are torn between belief and nonbelief, and 20 percent do not believe. Typically, children gradually relinquish this belief as they mature, passing from the belief stage to a transitional stage of uncertainty, in which they want to keep believing but are suspicious, to the final stage of disbelief.

When your child asks you a direct question about the reality of Santa, you should initially reply by asking, "Well, what do you think?" The child's answer may indicate that she or he is not ready for the truth but wants to know that it's O.K. to keep believing. If, however, your child's response reveals a serious doubt and a desire to know the truth, you should be honest. It can be very distressing and confusing to a child if you are deceptive when asked a serious question.

In stating the truth, you might say, "Well, dear, actually Santa Claus is just a pretend person—we told you this story because it's fun to imagine someone who brings toys even if he doesn't exist." You might add, "The spirit of Santa Claus does exist in the spirit of giving, caring, and joy in all of us. The spirit of giving comes from God, who is real."

Sometimes a problem exists because a child is willing to give up Santa Claus before the parents are. Many parents will continue to engage in practices supportive of the Santa myth even after it has become clear that the child no longer believes. As a result, older children may behave (as do their parents) as if Santa Claus exists even though they know he does not. This type of family myth undermines the kind of open, honest communication that is needed for psychologically healthy family functioning.

INDEX

153